Columbia University

Contributions to Education

Teachers College Series

No. 777

AMS PRESS
NEW YORK

DECISIONS AND ATTITUDES
AS OUTCOMES OF THE DISCUSSION
OF A SOCIAL PROBLEM

An Experimental Study

By WILLIAM MURRAY TIMMONS, Ph. D.

TEACHERS COLLEGE, COLUMBIA UNIVERSITY
CONTRIBUTIONS TO EDUCATION, NO. 777

Published with the Approval of
Professor Robert L. Thorndike, Sponsor

BUREAU OF PUBLICATIONS
TEACHERS COLLEGE, COLUMBIA UNIVERSITY
NEW YORK
1939

Library of Congress Cataloging in Publication Data

Timmons, William Murray, 1906-
    Decisions and attitudes as outcomes of the discussion
of a social problem.

    Reprint of the 1939 ed., issued in series: Teachers
College, Columbia University. Contributions to edu-
cation, no. 777.
    Originally presented as the author's thesis, Columbia.
    Bibliography: p.
    1. Attitude (Psychology) 2. Social problems.
3. Debates and debating. 4. Discussion. I. Title.
II. Series: Columbia University. Teachers College.
Contributions to education, no. 777.
BF323.C5T54 1972   301.15'43'3   75-177707

ISBN 0-404-55777-5

Reprinted by Special Arrangement with Teachers
College Press, New York, New York

From the edition of 1939, New York
First AMS edition published in 1972
Manufactured in the United States

AMS PRESS, INC.
NEW YORK, N. Y.   10003

ACKNOWLEDGMENTS

THE writer is deeply indebted to the many people who helped to make this study possible: To Professor Robert L. Thorndike, sponsor of the study, for continuous guidance and advice from the inception of the study to its completion; to Professor Lyman Bryson for suggesting the particular emphasis of the study; to Professor Irving Lorge, Professor Magdalene Kramer, Professor Helen Walker, and Professor Goodwin Watson for valuable criticisms. To Dr. F. Lovell Bixby, Chief of the Bureau of Probation and Parole, United States Department of Justice; Mr. William B. Cox, Executive Secretary of the Osborne Association; Attorney Sanford Bates; Commissioner William J. Ellis, New Jersey State Department of Institutions and Agencies; Mr. Winthrop D. Lane, Children's Bureau, United States Department of Labor; Professor E. H. Sutherland, University of Indiana; Professor James E. Hagerty, Ohio State University; Professor Thorsten Sellin, University of Pennsylvania; Professor Donald Taft, University of Illinois; Professor G. W. Sarvis, Ohio Wesleyan University; and Professor George B. Vold, University of Minnesota, for invaluable assistance in the preparation of experimental materials. The writer is particularly grateful to Dr. Bixby and Mr. Cox who gave a great deal of time. To Mrs. F. H. Bode, Mr. Jay R. Bone, Miss Kathryn Timmons, Dr. Thorndike, and my wife for assisting in the tedious work of rating the free expressions of attitude. To Superintendent Diener and Principal Stokes of Fremont (Ohio) Ross High School and to Superintendent Kinley and Principal Constien of Findlay (Ohio) High School for permission to experiment in their schools. To Messrs. Bone, Ballenger, McClintock, Huffman, Humphreys, Hochstettler, and Mattoon of the Fremont and Findlay schools for letting the experimenter work in their classes. The writer is particularly grateful to the many students in the Fremont and Findlay schools who willingly served as the subjects of the experiments.

W.M.T.

CONTENTS

CONTENTS

CHAPTER I

THE PROBLEM

THIS study represents an attempt to evaluate partially the assumption that discussion in addition to information is desirable for the wise decision on, and the appropriate attitude toward, a controversial social problem. More specifically, this study attempts to determine experimentally whether information on and discussion of a social problem cumulatively contribute to appropriate attitudes and appropriate solutions. Thus we are primarily concerned with some of the possible outcomes of discussion, outcomes in terms of the participant's attitudes and choices. In order to give the reader some orientation in the area being considered it appears advisable, before discussing the purpose of this research in detail, to outline very briefly possible outcomes of discussion, to discuss briefly influences which may produce such outcomes, and to consider the relationship of this study to previous experimental research.

POSSIBLE OUTCOMES OF DISCUSSION

The outcomes said to accrue from discussion are numerous. Whether they actually do accrue is not known in most cases, for in few instances have they been studied experimentally. The great majority of possible outcomes of discussion have been suggested by writers who, while having a wealth of experience with discussions, have not used an experimental attack. Inasmuch as in the present research interest centers primarily on outcomes of discussion in terms of the individual, only those suggested outcomes which pertain to the individual will be considered.

Many writers, for example, Judson [13],* suggest that discussion provides information and instruction. Others [23, 25, 30] assert that it permits the individual to see the point of view of

---

* Numbers in brackets refer to references given in the Bibliography, pp. 91-93.

others more clearly and with resulting tolerance. Sheffield [23] writes that discussion helps the participant form his conviction with some awareness of the forces that are at work in his own mind, that it shows him possibilities of putting group-tested convictions into practical effect. Lindeman [16] says that "discussion leads to a new orientation of interests. Moreover, by means of discussion the group comes to understand its specific interest and hence is better able to cooperate on its behalf." Elliott [6] and Follett [8, 9] both indicate that discussion produces ideally an integrated solution which is neither the acceptance of one point of view nor a compromise. Leigh [15] suggests a differing point of view: "A great deal of discussion represents, in reality, adoption by a group of the analysis made in advance by one of its members." Weise, Bryson, and Hallenbeck [35] indicate that discussion results in learning, clarification of thought, and the formation of more intelligent opinions. Sheffield [23] writes that it results in revised or readjusted personal attitudes and in adjustments of thought and feelings. Studebaker [30] writes that discussion is a "means by which all may become informed and active participants in carrying the responsibilities of government." Follett [8] says it provides a check on demagogy and propaganda. Other outcomes to the participant suggested by various authorities on the discussion process include the stimulation of understanding, the promotion of critical analysis, the development of critical thinking and the power of analysis, the provoking of interest in public affairs, the encouragement of reading, the resolution of conflict, the broadening of ideas, training in public speaking, the formation of new contacts and friendships, and catharsis.

In the present research we are interested in two of these possible outcomes: Does discussion result in better choices of solutions? And does it result in a revision of attitudes toward the problem? Implicit in many of the writings by authorities with wide practical experience in discussion is the belief that discussion does produce better decisions and more appropriate attitudes. For example, with reference to better decisions as an outcome Weise, Bryson, and Hallenbeck [35] write that when a man "makes his ideas and opinions all by himself, out of whole cloth, they can't be as good as when he takes the trouble to talk things over with others and compare his own reasons with theirs." With reference to attitude change as an outcome, Sheffield [23] writes that the outcome of discussion may be "revised personal attitudes looking to future action." It is the purpose of this study to test these beliefs experimentally.

POSSIBLE INFLUENCES PRODUCING DISCUSSION OUTCOMES

If such outcomes as those suggested really occur, they must be the result of certain dynamics, forces, or influences which occur in the discussion situation. It is not the task of this research to study these dynamics. Indeed, the forces at work presumably vary from discussion to discussion, depending probably upon the purpose of the discussion, the training of the participants, the nature of the problem, the interests involved, and many other factors. While the writer makes no attempt to state that the influences about to be mentioned actually occurred in the experimental discussions forming a large part of the present research, it is nevertheless probable that many or all of them were responsible for any outcomes which will be noted. One influence is undoubtedly active learning, that is, the recitation and active use of materials partly learned. Another probably is an averaging effect, the tendency for errors to cancel one another insofar as the errors are of a chance character [10, 14]. Still another influence is prestige [18, 27]. Later it will be noted that certain factual information was made available in the present experiment. The prestige of the author of the factual information may well have had a bearing on its acceptance and its use in arriving at decisions and attitudes. The influence of the majority opinion probably is involved in discussion. The existence of this factor is well-known and has been studied by such investigators as Moore [19] and Thorndike [32]. The increased range of suggestions leading toward a solution is probably an additional influence at work in the discussion situation. The varied interpretations of facts and experiences found in a group appear to give the group a better opportunity to arrive at the most appropriate interpretations. Coupled with this influence is the wider range of criticism of suggestions and interpretations found in the group. Shaw [22] found that rejections of erroneous suggestions were generally made by group members other than the one who made the suggestion. Insofar as criticism occurs in the discussion, it is probable that discussion provides a basis for critical rejection of inadequate suggestions and interpretations, a basis much wider than that found when an individual works alone. An additional influence at work in the group is undoubtedly the information held by the various members of the group and not held by other members. Still other influences which may or may not be to the advantage of discussion are argumentative and persuasive techniques, individual personality characteristics, the size of the group, emotional attachment to suggestions, the training and experience of the participants, the type of leadership, and the nature of the task.

It should be noted that some of these influences could exist without discussion occurring; they are not peculiar to the discussion situation. Such influences include active learning, the aggregation or averaging of individual contributions, and the prestige of majorities or individuals. Insofar as these influence the outcomes of discussion, one cannot hold that the results are due to the discussion. However, insofar as such influences as range of suggestions, interpretations, and criticism are present, the outcomes may be due to factors inherent in the discussion situation.

EXPERIMENTAL RESEARCH IN DISCUSSION

It has been indicated that the present research is concerned with two possible outcomes of discussion, outcomes in terms of the participant's attitudes and solutions. Previous experimental research that has considered outcomes in terms of the individual is limited. Several studies have demonstrated that increased or better output in terms of *product* results from discussion. The studies of Thorndike [31, 32], Simpson [25], Dashiell [5], South [28], Shaw [22], Watson [33, 34], Bechterev and Lange [3], and Jenness [12] are of this sort. Burt [4] found that changes in product due to discussion were in the wrong direction about as often as in the right. South's results [28] varied with the nature of the task. A few studies have considered outcome in terms of the *individual*. Gurnee [11] found group learning superior to average individual learning. Simpson [25] found that the discussion of esthetic problems improved students' subsequent esthetic judgments. Spence [29], working with graduate students in a course in educational psychology, found more improvement in learning following a series of lectures than following a series of class discussions. Bane [1] found that college classes taught by the discussion method were superior in delayed recall to similar classes taught by the lecture method. Barton [2] found that discussing students were superior in problem-solving ability in algebra to similar students who worked individually. Barton, however, did not compute the reliability of the differences. When computed by the writer, for neither test used was the difference significant, the critical ratios being only slightly more than one. From this brief review of previous experimental research in discussion it is apparent that little emphasis has been placed on outcomes in terms of the individual. Where such outcomes have been considered, they have had to do with learning, recall, and problem solving. The majority of the outcomes in terms of the individual which have been suggested as resulting from discussion have not been studied experimentally. No experimental studies have, to the writer's knowledge, considered the outcomes which the present study considers, the participant's attitudes and solutions.

As indicated above the present research is concerned with these outcomes when the problem for discussion is a controversial social problem. By a controversial social problem the writer means a social problem which cannot be solved satisfactorily by measurement or by reference to accepted concepts, definitions, or systems. It is doubtful that this investigation type can be satisfactorily solved by discussion. Certainly, actual measurement or reference to accepted concepts, definitions, or systems provides a better solution. For the controversial social problem as here considered the best solution that one can obtain at this time is based on a consensus of expert judgment. This is not to say that information is unimportant, for without doubt the expert judgment is based on wide information. Previous experimental researches have used for the most part experimental tasks very different from that which this study terms the controversial social problem. In order to be certain of the correct solution, the tasks used were most often of a factual nature: the selection of true facts from false, the completion of sentences, vocabulary tests, puzzles, word building, comparison of numbers, and estimating the number of beans in a bottle. Some of the tasks used were complex, for example, Shaw's puzzles [22] and Watson's [33] decoding a cipher and listing steps to solve a problem. Few of them, however, permitted much interchange of ideas and opinions. Furthermore, they aroused, presumably, very little of the emotional bias with which persons characteristically approach life situations. Of the tasks used in previous experimental research those involving esthetic judgments, such as those of Simpson [25], perhaps are most closely analogous to lifelike situations. But esthetic judgments are matters of taste and not very susceptible to verbalization and discussion. They probably have less of a rational basis than do most real life problems. In any event, they are not controversial social problems.

PURPOSE OF THE STUDY

It has been stated that this study represents an attempt to evaluate partially the assumption that discussion in addition to information is desirable for the wise decision on and the appropriate attitude toward a controversial social problem. It attempts to determine experimentally whether information on and discussion of a social problem cumulatively contribute to appropriate attitudes and appropriate solutions. We are concerned with whether those who discuss do any better in these respects than do similar individuals who devote the discussing time to individual restudy. This problem connotes that students are given information on a social problem at one stage of an experiment. At a second stage part of them discuss while the others, control subjects, restudy the information. Appropriate measures of attitude and of solution are administered before and after each stage of the experiment and, in order that retention may be measured, again at a later date.

Specific questions for which answers are sought include:

A. Questions pertaining to the effect of information and discussion on choice of solution to the social problem:

1. After information alone is available are there changes in choice of solution in the direction of the good choice?
2. Are there additional changes in the direction of the good solution after discussion of the social problem?
3. Are there additional changes in the direction of the good solution after restudy of the information?
4. Do those who study only differ significantly in choice of solution from those who study and discuss?
5. Do the individuals who study and discuss retain their choices of solution as well as those who study only?

B. Questions pertaining to the effect of information and discussion on attitude toward the social problem:

1. After information alone is available are there changes in the direction of the appropriate attitude toward the social problem?
2. Are there additional changes in the direction of the good attitude after discussion of the social problem?
3. Are there additional changes in the direction of the good attitude after restudy of the information?
4. Do those who study only differ significantly in attitude from those who study and discuss?
5. Do the individuals who study and discuss retain their attitudes as well as those who study and restudy?

The review of previous researches indicates that these questions have not been studied experimentally. Few of these researches considered outcomes in terms of the individual, none in terms of attitudes and decisions. No previous study known to the writer has considered such outcomes when the experimental task was a controversial life-like problem.

CHAPTER II

THE PROCEDURE

INTRODUCTION

SINCE the purpose of this study was to determine experimentally whether information on and discussion of a social problem cumulatively contribute to appropriate changes of attitude and appropriate choices of solution, the following aspects of the procedure should be considered in some detail: (1) determining the problem to be discussed; (2) selecting, constructing, and rating tools of measurement and other experimental materials; and (3) conducting the experiment. Each of these procedural steps will in turn be considered in the following pages. At the end of the chapter the types of data secured will be listed and the limitations of the research discussed.

DETERMINING THE PROBLEM TO BE DISCUSSED

In determining the experimental task, the problem to be studied and discussed, the writer had several criteria in mind. The problem must be controversial. It should be the sort of problem on which people in real life situations disagree. Furthermore, it should be considered worthy of serious discussion. It should not be a task involving the determination of a fact or the solution of a puzzle. In addition, if the purpose of the study were to be fulfilled, the problem must be one for which the appropriate solution —the good answer—is determinable. It should be one on which the experimental subjects would presumably be poorly informed, on which the popular solutions might well be wrong. Finally, it should be within the average experimental subject's range of interest and comprehension. It should be complex without being abstruse.

Controversial problems and problems meeting all criteria except one were readily found. Those for which the good decision could be determined were extremely rare. It soon became obvious that one would have to rely for the good answer on a consensus of expert judgment if a controversial task for which the good answer was determinable were to be used.

The experimental task was finally chosen by narrowing consideration to the few problems found on which well informed individuals might be expected to agree. In order to learn whether the experts showed any agreement on these problems, wide reading followed. Two problems on which the experts apparently agreed, parole and trade barriers among the states, were found. The one dealing with parole was tentatively selected because the investigator felt it would have more interest to the experimental subjects, although either problem would apparently have met all of the criteria. To be sure that experts agreed on the solution to the parole problem, the writer polled, as discussed below, a number of experts—all considered by their colleagues as the most competent academic and non-academic criminologists and sociologists in the area of the experimental task. The problem as finally selected was: "What, if anything, should be done about Ohio's system of releasing convicts from prison?" To make sure that it was within the comprehension and interests of the subjects to be used, it was first presented to a similar group of individuals. This trial showed that such students comprehended the problem and that they were readily interested in it.

SELECTING, CONSTRUCTING, AND RATING THE EXPERIMENTAL MATERIALS

If the purpose of the study were to be fulfilled, measures (1) of attitude toward the general problem, (2) of solution to the problem, and (3) of ability to evaluate the characteristics of solutions were necessary. A standard of *goodness* for each of these measures had to be set. In addition, a method of informing the subjects had to be selected and materials prepared.

Measures of Attitude. Not only a measure of attitude but also an object of reference for that measure had to be selected. Since parole systems vary in their goodness, the *best parole system known to the student* was arbitrarily selected as the object of reference. This object of reference is admittedly somewhat vague. It is possible that the *best* system might vary from subject to subject and from measure to measure. The alternative of using *parole systems* as the object of reference, however, is open to the same criticisms. A trial use of the Remmers-Kelley generalized "Scale for Measuring Attitude toward Any Institution" [21] proved its sensitiveness in detecting changes in attitude toward the best parole system resulting from the students' reading of materials on parole. Consequently, it was selected as the measure of attitude.

The *good* attitude was a consensus of experts' attitudes toward the best parole system known. Nine experts (two of them twice) checked copies of the Remmers-Kelley scale. Those who checked two forms of the scale were given a score which was the average of their two scores. The scores thus obtained ranged from 8.8 to 9.8, with a mean of 9.3. This score, then, represented the good attitude. The experts' mean attitude was definitely favorable toward the best parole system but short of being extremely favorable. The *best* to the experts was hardly ideal.

The Remmers-Kelley scale was scored as follows: Inasmuch as in this study interest is focused on the individual's score in relation to the experts' mean score, which is assumed to be the good attitude, the experts' mean score was given a value of zero. All other scores then became plus, zero, or minus values, ranging from —7.7 to 1.9.

Subsequent use of the Remmers-Kelley scale created doubt concerning its ability to discriminate slight changes in attitude at the positive end of the scale. As a result, another measure of attitude was used with a second group of subjects. This second measure involved having each student at each stage of the experiment give in one sentence a free expression of attitude toward the best parole system known to him. These expressions were then rated by judges on a ten-point scale of favorableness-unfavorableness to the best parole system.

Three competent judges rated 1330 such expressions of attitude. The following instructions were given each judge:

Rating Expressions of Attitude. On the accompanying three by five cards are students' free expressions of attitude toward the best parole system. You are asked to rate these free expressions of attitude on a ten-point scale of favorableness-unfavorableness to the best parole system. Let *1* represent the expressions which are most *unfavorable* to the best parole system; let *10* represent the expressions which are most *favorable* to the best parole system. (Neutral opinions will not necessarily be rated at the mid-points *5* or *6*.) The intermediate points on the scale will then represent intermediate attitudes of favorableness-unfavorableness. The object of the rating is to arrange the cards into ten approximately equal piles, each representing a point on the ten-point scale.

It is suggested that the following procedure be followed: First, read over a number of samples to get an idea of the range of opinion expressed. Then, make a preliminary sorting into ten piles, the pile on the extreme left representing the most unfavorable attitudes toward the best parole system and the pile on the extreme right representing the most favorable attitudes toward the best parole system. After the preliminary sorting is completed, revise the piles (1) to make the number of cards in each approximately equal and (2) to readjust any cards that now seem to be in the wrong pile.

If some of the statements on the cards seem ambiguous and inappropriate to you, remember that they are unrevised student expressions and as such many of them may be expected to be somewhat lacking in clarity. Do the best you can with them. Those which are ambiguous or inappropriate will in part be determined by the differing placement of such statements by the various raters.

The correlations between the ratings (based on a sample of 247 cards selected at random) were as follows:

Judges A and B	$r = .87$	$PE_r = .012$
Judges B and C	$r = .82$	$PE_r = .015$
Judges A and C	$r = .81$	$PE_r = .015$

If the median correlation, .82, is taken to represent the correlations of all three judges and if it is corrected by the Spearman-Brown formula, the correlation becomes .93. Thus the ratings of the judges were sufficiently similar for a consideration of the attitudes of groups of subjects.

The standard of goodness in this measure of attitude was de-

termined in the following way: Twelve free expressions of attitude were collected from the highly informed experts. These were
placed among the 1330 student expressions and rated by the
judges on the same ten-point scale. In order to be particularly
certain of the experts' standard, a sample of 100 student expressions distributed at every point on the scale by the three judges
was selected. To these the experts' expressions were again added.
The new sample of 112 cards was then rated by three additional
judges, according to the same plan used previously for the 1330
expressions. The average rating of the experts' expressions then
became the good attitude. This average for the first three judges
was 7.59. When the ratings by the three additional judges were
added, the mean became 7.60. The standard deviation of the distribution was 1.46, the standard error of the mean 0.17. The additional ratings, it will be noted, resulted in practically no change
in the mean of the experts' rated attitudes. The mean presumably
would remain fairly constant even if many additional ratings
were made. We can be practically certain, in any event, that the
true mean rating lies between 7.09 and 8.11. This mean experts'
attitude represented on the ten-point scale a fairly positive attitude. The experts considered the best parole system good but not
ideal.

When the first three judges' combined ratings for these 112
cards are compared with the second three judges' ratings, the resulting r is .98 with a PE_r of .006. This is a closer relationship
than that predicted by the Spearman-Brown formula. Consequently, we can be fairly sure that the ratings are sufficiently
reliable.

For computations the free expressions of attitude were scored
as follows: The experts' mean score, 7.6 as determined by the
ten-point rating, was given a value of zero. The students' scores,
determined in the same rating of the free expressions, then were
zero or plus or minus the zero point. To facilitate computations
the ratings of the student expressions were totaled rather than
averaged. Since three judges had rated all student expressions,
the score values ranged from three to thirty. In order to place the
experts' standard on the same basis the mean of the experts' scores

was multiplied by three. The good attitude then had a score value of 22.8.

Measure of Solutions. A measure of choice of solution was also needed. This measure might consider one solution right, all others wrong. On the other hand, various solutions might be considered as having varying degrees of goodness. From another point of view students might be asked to frame their own solutions to the problem, or they might be asked to choose from given alternatives. In order that the choices and shifts in choices might be readily scored, the method of having the students choose from given alternatives was selected. And so that there might be more basis for discussion, the given solutions were to have varying degrees of goodness. Five alternative solutions to the experimental task were finally used. Each was to be ranked by the experimental subjects. These five were selected from a group of fifteen rated by a group of highly informed experts. Six experts agreed closely in their rating of seven of the submitted solutions. Five of the seven solutions seemed to fall at different points of the scale. These five were selected for trial use. The trial showed that the wording of some was inadvisable, causing them on the initial measurement to be ranked on the basis of their wording. The five were then reworded and again submitted to the experts, this time for ranking in the order of goodness. Five experts, four of whom had not rated the other solutions, agreed exactly in their rankings. A sixth expert made one inversion, a choice which he qualified in an accompanying letter. A total of eleven experts, then, were in essential agreement on the ranking of the five solutions. The alternative solutions used are a part of the Ranking Sheet reproduced below.

Name............... Date.......... Course............

RANKING SHEET

Directions: Below are five possible solutions to the problem: *What, if anything, should be done about Ohio's method of releasing convicts from prison?* You are asked to rank these solutions on the basis of what you now know and believe. Place your rankings in the blanks provided to the left of the solutions. In the blank to the left of the solution which you consider *best,* write the numeral "1." In the blank to the left of the solution which you consider *second best,* write the numeral "2." In the blank to the left of the solution which you consider *third best,* write the numeral "3." In the blank to the left of the solution which you consider *fourth best,* write the numeral "4." In the blank to the left of the solution which you consider *fifth best* (worst), write the numeral "5." Give a different rank to each solution; rank all five. Consider the listed solutions only. Do not in any way change their wording; consider them as stated.

Rankings	*Solutions*
......	A. Ohio should keep its present system of releasing prisoners.
......	B. Ohio should adopt the essential aspects of the New York system of releasing prisoners.
......	C. Ohio should adopt the Mississippi system of releasing prisoners.
......	D. Ohio should adopt the New Jersey system of releasing prisoners.
......	E. Ohio should keep its present system of releasing prisoners, adding only a scheme whereby the releasing authorities have complete data on all prisoners eligible for release.

(BE SURE YOUR NAME IS AT THE TOP OF THIS PAGE.)

The Ranking Sheets were scored in the following manner: The student's ranking of the five alternative solutions was compared with the experts' ranking. Then the differences between the student's ranking and the experts' ranking were noted. For example:

Experts' Ranking	Student's Ranking	Difference	Difference Squared
4	3	1	1
2	2	0	
5	4	1	1
1	1	0	
3	5	2	4
		Sum 4	Sum 6

Now if these differences were merely summed as in column three the student making rankings far different from the experts' would not be sufficiently penalized. Consequently, in scoring the differences have been squared and summed just as they are in computing correlation by the rank-difference method. The score on the Ranking Sheet, then, was the sum of the squared differences between the student's ranking and that of the experts.

Evaluation of Characteristics of Solutions. The test evaluating the characteristics of solutions, termed an "Information Test" for the students' benefit, was constructed by collecting thirty-two characteristics of the various systems of releasing convicts from prison. These were submitted to nine experts with instructions to place a plus sign before each statement representing an important characteristic of a good system, a minus sign before each statement representing an undesirable characteristic of a good system, and a zero before any representing neither desirable nor undesirable characteristics. Any statement on which more than one of the nine experts disagreed was removed from the test. The nine experts were in perfect agreement on twenty-four statements; one dissented on each of six other statements. Two statements were eliminated, leaving thirty statements in the test. This test, reproduced below, was used on the third day of the experiment with one group of students only.

The test evaluating the characteristics of solutions was scored in the following manner: For each item marked incorrectly one point was deducted from the perfect score of thirty.

Name .... Course and Period ....
Date ....

INFORMATION TEST

Directions: Below are listed a number of characteristics of methods of releasing convicts from prison. Before each one you consider an important characteristic of a *good* method of releasing convicts from prison place a plus sign. Before each one you consider detrimental to a good method of releasing convicts from prison place a minus sign. Before any item which you consider neither important nor detrimental place a zero.

1. The prison sentences are for the most part indeterminate.
2. Prison sentences are mainly determinate.
3. The releasing authorities are distinct from the prison authorities, each group adopting its own policies and procedures.
4. Prison and release policies and procedures are planned by one government agency.
5. Policy-making officials have relatively long terms of office which are staggered so that not all members retire from office at the same time.
6. All officials and employees, save for parole board members or policy-making boards, are under civil service.
7. The permanent officials are trained in prison, parole, and welfare work.
8. All officials are given office and hold office without regard to politics.
9. Officials are political friends of the appointing authorities.
10. Prison guards are trusted prisoners.
11. The education, work, and recreation of the convict while in prison are preparation for eventual release.
12. The first qualification of work for the convict while in prison is reduced cost to the state of keeping the prisoners.
13. Treatment in prison is punishment so that the convict will "go straight" when released.
14. Every new convict in prison is studied by doctors, psychologists, educators, etc., with the purpose of arriving at a program of training for the convict.
15. While in prison the convict's progress is checked periodically by experts.
16. When a convict has served his definite sentence, he is automatically released without supervision.
17. The releasing board normally does not have available social case histories and psychological reports of the convict eligible for release.
18. Before releasing a convict the board which has the power to release has available experts' reports of progress in prison, experts' reports of home and community conditions, and psychological or psychiatric reports.
19. Generally, release depends on employment for the convict.
20. Released prisoners are supervised.
21. Officials supervising released prisoners are themselves guided and directed by their superiors.
22. Officials who supervise released convicts secure their training through experience.

23. Officials supervising released convicts follow their own systems of supervision.
24. During the first weeks of release a convict is seen frequently by a supervising official.
25. Supervising officials make detailed systematic reports on released convicts to a central office.
26. A supervising official has no more released convicts to supervise than he can readily see as often as is necessary.
27. The officials supervising released convicts have nothing to do with the systematic reporting of the released prisoner.
28. Supervision, even technical supervision, extends beyond one year for cause only.
29. Once released a convict is rarely seen by a supervising official.
30. A released prisoner may be returned to prison without trial for breaking any rule or condition of his release.

Information Pamphlet. One of the experimental factors had to do with change of attitude and choice of solution as a result of the availability of information. Consequently, a method of making information available had to be decided upon. A body of factual information about parole systems and other systems of releasing convicts from prison could be presented orally or in written form. Since the written form could be presented to all subjects more uniformly and could be available for reference, that method was selected.

A body of factual information covering the systems involved in the alternative solutions was then compiled from the writings on the subject, from interviews with experts, and from correspondence with experts. In the pamphlet thus constructed no statement of opinion about any system was included. Competent academic and non-academic criminologists and sociologists reviewed the pamphlet for accuracy and completeness. The pamphlet was then used with a small group of students similar to the experimental subjects. The purpose of the trial was to learn whether the language and concepts used were sufficiently simple and clear. A few minor changes were made at the suggestion of the experts and the trial students. The pamphlet is reproduced in the appendix to this volume.

A report form for the discussion groups, except for instructions an adaptation of the Ranking Sheet, was also constructed. It is reproduced later in this chapter.

CONDUCTING EXPERIMENT A

Two similar experiments were conducted in two high schools in northwestern Ohio. The two experiments will be referred to as A and B. As has been indicated earlier, the materials and procedure used varied slightly in the two experiments. As a result, the procedure used in the first school will be discussed first, then that of the second school. For subjects of both experiments psychological test scores were available. These were secured well in advance of the experiment so that control classes would be known to be roughly equal to experimental classes in general ability. The scores were from the Ohio State University Psychological Test, Form 20.

The subjects of Experiment A were 334 high school juniors and seniors enrolled in required courses in American history and social problems. Two hundred sixty-five of these were experimental subjects; the remaining 69 served as controls on the one day that controls were needed. The 265 experimental subjects had a mean score of 54.89 on the psychological test. The standard deviation of the distribution was 23.6, the standard error of the mean 1.45. On the same test the 69 control students had a mean score of 54.72. The standard deviation of the distribution was 24.7, the standard error of the mean 2.95. Thus in general ability as measured by the Ohio State University Psychological Test, Form 20 the two groups were approximately equal.

Three consecutive class meetings were necessary for the experiment proper. One month later a fourth class meeting was used. The procedure for the control students differed from that for the experimentals on the third day only. The class meetings in Experiment A were fifty-five minutes in length. Not all of the period was used by the experimenter on the first and fourth days.

First Day. On the first day all students, both experimental and control, had the same experiences. The experiment was introduced, the attitude scale and the Ranking Sheet were administered, and a final comment was made.

In order to secure the students' cooperation the following introduction to the experiment was made extemporaneously:

For three days we shall be conducting an experiment. We shall try to find out—with your help—how much your beliefs on a social problem change as a result of reading and discussing certain facts about the problem. No grade will be involved. You will have no home work to do. We insist that you do no home work. We shall, however, expect you to do as well as you can everything asked of you. Under no circumstances should you talk with any one outside the classroom (your fellow students, other students, or parents) about the experiment or the materials used until after the third day. If you talk with others, we shall be unable to tell how the experiment comes out. After the third day you may talk with any one except your instructor for as long as you wish. In about a month the experimenter will return to tell you the results of the experiment.

The attitude scale was disguised on the first day by having the students indicate their attitudes toward labor unions and the best sales tax system as well as toward the best parole system. After the scales were distributed, the experimenter read aloud the directions printed on the scales. "Labor unions," "sales tax," and "parole system" were defined, the last as a "system whereby convicts are released from prison under a greater or lesser amount of supervision." The scales were then marked and collected.

The third step on the first day was administering the Ranking Sheet, a copy of which was reproduced earlier in this chapter. On this occasion this sheet, like the attitude scale, was disguised by adding alternative solutions to the labor union and sales tax problems. Again the directions were read aloud to the students. Every precaution was taken on the first day to be sure that the students understood what was to be done.

After the ranking sheets were marked and collected, a final comment was made: The students were reminded that they were to talk with no one about the content of the experiment until after the third day.

Second Day. The procedure on the second day was again the same for all students, experimental and control. After a brief talk to motivate cooperation, the information pamphlets were distributed. The printed instructions were read aloud to the students. They were told that they had all but the final ten minutes of the class period in which to study the pamphlet. The pamphlet and the instructions are found in the Appendix. Throughout the period the students were observed closely to see that they were reading. Almost every student read or studied for the full forty minutes allowed.

During the final ten minutes of the period the attitude scale and the Ranking Sheet were again administered, this time without the experimenter's reading the instructions. At the close of the period the students were again asked to do no talking about the problem with anyone until the conclusion of the experiment.

Third Day, Experimental Subjects. On the third day the experimental classes followed a procedure different from that followed by the control classes. In the experimental classes discussion and the composition of the discussion groups were first announced. Then the students were divided into groups of four, without regard to sex, on the basis of the previous day's ranking scores. The distribution of the second day's ranking scores had been divided into three segments, the students having the best scores (0–2) being termed *good,* those having intermediate scores (4–14) *intermediate,* and those having poor scores (16 and up) *poor.* With these three types of subject six types of group with reference to second day's ranking scores were formed. According to their composition these types are indicated below:

Type	Group Composition
I	4 subjects with good scores
II	4 subjects with intermediate scores
III	4 subjects with poor scores
IV	2 subjects with good scores; 2 subjects with poor scores
V	2 subjects with good scores; 2 subjects with intermediate scores
VI	2 subjects with intermediate scores; 2 subjects with poor scores

The students, of course, had no knowledge of the group composition.

After the groups were formed in designated parts of the room, Group Instruction and Report Sheets, Reasons Sheets, and information pamphlets were distributed, one of each to each group. Copies of the first two are reproduced below.

The instructions on the Group Instruction and Report Sheet were then read aloud by the experimenter, who added the comment that the greatest difficulty in such discussions was not the noise (for there was surprisingly little considering that there were often eight groups discussing in an average-sized classroom) but the tendency for those who disagreed to get into "yes-no" battles. It was suggested that disagreements were best resolved by having each person state his reasons and letting the others criticize them. The purpose of the discussions, of course, was to arrive at group rankings.

Having the groups list (on the Reasons Sheet) the considerations upon which their rankings were based tended, it was thought, to cause the students to take the task seriously and to avoid arriving without thought at a ranking.

One information pamphlet only was supplied each group. This procedure was followed in order to insure cooperative work and to prevent the subjects from reading while they should be participating in the discussion. However, the experimenter desired that the information be available in order to eliminate lengthy discussion of what the facts were and to facilitate the students' getting quickly to the evaluation of the facts.

Group chairmen were not appointed. As above, the experimenter desired to encourage cooperative action. Approximately thirty-eight minutes were allowed for the discussions. Ten minutes before the end of the period the group reports were collected and the attitude scale and the ranking sheet were again administered to the students as individuals.

GROUP INSTRUCTION AND REPORT SHEET

Group Type .... Members of the Group: ....
Course ....
Period ....
....
....

INSTRUCTIONS FOR DISCUSSION GROUPS
(Read this page carefully.)

Below are five solutions to the problem: *What, if anything, should be done about Ohio's method of releasing convicts from prison?* As individuals you have already ranked these solutions. Today, your *group* through discussion will rank them. Do the ranking on the basis of the factual information which you read yesterday. Feel free to refer to the information pamphlet at any time during the discussion. Remember, however, that discussion begins after you know the facts. What do the facts mean? Do they mean that system "A" is better than system "B" or that the systems are merely different?

By talking things over, by evaluating the facts, and by weighing and criticizing one another's suggestions and reasons, attempt to come to a group agreement as to which solution is best, which second best, and so forth. If it is impossible to agree, turn in a majority report and a minority report. In most cases you will be able to agree if you discuss thoroughly. Considering "1" best, "2" second best, "3" third best, "4" fourth best, and "5" fifth best (worst), place your group rankings in the blanks to the left of the solutions.

On the next page in the space given list the reasons for each ranking made. If, when listing these reasons, you decide that there are insufficient reasons for the ranking given a solution, feel free to select another solution for which you can determine better reasons.

In brief, your *group* is to do two things:

(1) Through discussion *rank* the five solutions stated below.
(2) For each solution give the reasons for the ranking.

RANKINGS OF SOLUTIONS

Rankings   *Solutions*

(Consider these solutions only. Do not in any way change
their wording. Consider them as stated.)

....   A. Ohio should keep its present system of releasing prisoners.

....   B. Ohio should adopt the essential aspects of the New York system of releasing prisoners.

....   C. Ohio should adopt the Mississippi system of releasing prisoners.

....   D. Ohio should adopt the New Jersey system of releasing prisoners.

....   E. Ohio should keep its present system of releasing prisoners, adding only a scheme whereby the releasing authorities have complete data on all prisoners eligible for release.

(Are names at top of this sheet the names of the members of your group?)

Group Type ....   Members of the Group............
Course ....
Period ....
                                         ....

REASONS FOR MAKING EACH CHOICE
(Be brief but clear. Use complete sentences.)

Solution .... (indicate the letter) is the *best* solution for the following reasons:

Solution .... is the *second best* solution for the following reasons:

Solution .... is the *third best* solution for the following reasons:

Solution .... is the *fourth best* solution for the following reasons:

Solution .... is the *fifth best* (worst) solution for the following reasons:

Minority Report: If you find that through discussion the group cannot come to an agreement in ranking the solutions, ask for another report form. Then the majority report will be placed on this blank and the minority report on the new form.

Third Day, Control Subjects. While the experimental students were discussing, the control students restudied the information pamphlet. In order to motivate the additional study, the experimenter suggested that they were competing with those classes that were discussing. He also suggested that each student should take notes on each section of the pamphlet so that he might be better able to rank the solutions intelligently. Even with these suggestions some of the students did not study the pamphlet for all of the forty minutes allowed. Some felt that they had secured all they could from the pamphlet in less time. There is no doubt that the control students would have preferred discussing to the additional study of the pamphlet. Crestfallen expressions greeted the experimenter when he announced additional study. By and large, however, it is the writer's opinion that the control students co-operated very well. During the last ten minutes of the period the ranking sheet and the attitude scale were again administered.

Fourth Day. On the fourth day, after an interval of one month, in order to test the retention of attitudes and rankings of solutions the attitude scale and the ranking sheet were once again administered to all students, control and experimental.

CONDUCTING EXPERIMENT B

Experiment B, conducted in a city near that in which Experiment A was conducted, included 338 subjects, 144 serving as controls. These students were seniors enrolled in a required course in American history and juniors and seniors enrolled in an elective course in sociology. The Ohio State University Psychological Test, Form 20 scores for the 194 experimental students had a mean of 62.05. The standard deviation of the distribution was 25.0, the standard error of the mean 1.8. The 144 control students had a mean score of 60.48. The standard deviation of the distribution was 26.4, the standard error of the mean 2.2. These experimental and control students were apparently superior in general ability to the students of Experiment A. Two factors probably account for the difference. A larger proportion of those in Experiment B were seniors. City B also probably has a somewhat more selected population than City A. In most essentials Experiment B was the same as Experiment A. The differences were:

1. The class periods were forty-five minutes in length, ten minutes shorter than in Experiment A.

2. The Remmers-Kelley scale was omitted; a free expression of attitude was substituted.

3. On the second day five minutes less time was allowed for reading the information pamphlet.

4. On the third day the experimental students had approximately twenty-eight minutes for discussion, ten minutes fewer than did the corresponding students in Experiment A.

5. At the end of the third day the test of ability to evaluate the

characteristics of methods of releasing convicts from prison was added.

6. On the third day the control students were asked to prepare a column on paper for each of the systems considered in the information pamphlet. In the upper half of each column they were asked to list the good points of the system, in the lower half the bad points.

7. The measures of attitude and of solution were used undisguised on the first day in Experiment B. The students in Experiment A had been disgruntled at being fooled, at not being trusted, and at not being permitted to discuss the other problems.

A larger proportion of the students in Experiment B were used as control students because the addition of the evaluation of characteristics test made possible an additional comparison between the experimental and the control students. Since greater dependence would thus be placed on the control group, a larger proportion of the students was placed in that group.

The free expression of attitude was substituted for the Remmers-Kelley scale at every stage of the experiment where that scale was used in Experiment A. The substitution occurred because of certain doubts concerning the ability of the scale to discriminate small positive changes after an attitude had become fairly positive. This matter will be further discussed when the data on attitudes are presented.

Free expressions of attitude were secured by the following oral instructions:

Parole, as you probably know, is a method by which prisoners who have served a part of their prison sentences are released from prison under supervision. On the basis of this definition and on the basis of what you now know (however little or much that may be), indicate in a brief declarative sentence what you think of the best parole system of which you know. Let this sentence express accurately your present feelings toward the best parole system, remembering that the best may be very good, very bad, or very ordinary. Let your sentence take some such form as the following samples:

1. It is the best possible method of releasing convicts.
2. The world could not exist without it.

3. It develops the parolee's character.
4. It helps the released convict meet economic problems.
5. It encourages moral improvement.
6. It is fundamentally sound.
7. It is necessary as a means of controlling crime.
8. Its good and bad points balance.
9. It is unfair to the released prisoner.
10. It is developing into a racket.
11. It has positively no value.

Do not write that System A is the best. You need not name the system you are thinking of. Just tell me what you think of the best system. In many cases you may well commence your sentence with the words "it is." Do not select one of the sentences read. They are merely samples of the sort of sentence you are to write. Construct a sentence—one sentence only—which best expresses your present opinion. Write this sentence near the bottom of the Ranking Sheet.

Complete instructions were given the first time free expressions of attitude were desired. On subsequent occasions the same instructions were condensed to a few sentences. While the students were filling out the Ranking Sheet and writing the expressions of attitude, the experimenter observed as closely as possible to see that they were following the instructions and not writing sentences such as "It is the best," "Texas has the best system," and so forth.

The feature of requesting the control students on the day of the restudy to note in columns the good and the poor points of each system was added to make more certain that the control students really gave the pamphlet additional study while the experimental students were discussing.

DATA SECURED

The use of the materials, measures, and procedures described above made available the several types of data indicated below. Except in the one instance noted, all types of data were available for the subjects of both experiments:

1. Psychological test scores.
2. Initial attitude and ranking scores.

3. Attitude and ranking scores after an opportunity to reread the pamphlet.
4. Attitude and ranking scores of the experimental students after discussion and the same scores of the control students after an opportunity to restudy the information pamphlet.
5. Group ranking scores of the experimental students after discussion.
6. Scores on the test of ability to evaluate the characteristics of solutions for the experimental students after discussion and for the control students after restudy of the information pamphlet (Experiment B only).
7. Attitude and ranking scores one month after the completion of the experiment proper.

In analyzing these data three statistical devices were ordinarily used: (a) the reliability of the mean change technique, (b) the reliability of the difference between mean change technique, and (c) the Pearson product-moment r. The reliability of the mean change technique dispensed with the use of r in determining the reliability of any change from one stage of the experiment to another. Instead of using the scores themselves *changes* in scores were used. The mean change divided by the standard error of the mean change gave an index of reliability. Since, in determining the reliability of the difference between mean changes, there was in no instance any correlation between the two series of scores, the simple formula $\sigma_{diff} = \sqrt{\sigma m_1^2 + \sigma m_2^2}$ was always used. The Pearson r was used for every correlation computation. Where other techniques were used, a discussion of the technique accompanies the exposition of its use. The nature of the data analyses will be considered in detail in the succeeding chapters.

LIMITATIONS OF THE RESEARCH

Before closing this chapter which has described the materials, measures, and procedures of the experiments, the writer will consider briefly some of the limitations of the research. The findings presented on subsequent pages must be considered with reference to these limitations.

In the first place, the conclusions made are limited to the type of population used as experimental subjects—young adults without formal training in discussion techniques. The results might well be different for different populations or for populations trained in discussion techniques. The results might well be different if the discussers had competent leaders rather than having to grope about to the best of their ability. Furthermore, the results might well be more favorable to the discussing students if less intensive pressure were put on the control students at the time of restudy.

The findings are applicable to one type of discussion only, the type in which the participants select a solution from several given alternatives. The results may have little application to the type of discussion which seeks a new solution to the problem presented.

In the type of discussion used in this study the range of possible response is admittedly limited. The person or group responding is not permitted any other solution than one of the five given alternatives. It is true, of course, that such limitations of response occur very often in real life situations; for example, in voting in an election. In such a case one is often faced with choosing from alternatives, none of which he can wholeheartedly approve. Nevertheless, he attempts to select the best of the given choices. If the subjects of the experiment had been permitted to frame their own solutions, there would have been a serious practical difficulty in scoring shifts in choices of solution. There would also have been the practical problem of informing the students on a much wider range of methods of dealing with convicts. These two considerations caused the experimenter to present the five alternative solutions.

A fourth limitation has to do with using experts to determine the *good* attitude and the relative *goodness* of the solutions. It may be said that the experts arrived at their decisions and attitudes on the basis of information and discussion generally similar to the information and discussion experienced by the subjects of the experiment. It may be maintained, then, that the shifts in attitude and solution found experimentally were not shifts with reference to the *good* attitude and decision but shifts with reference to *an* attitude and decision based on similar facts and similar discussion. The writer does not consider this a serious limitation. The experts' attitudes and solutions were undoubtedly the result of much information, experience, observation, and discussion extending over a long period of time. Their attitudes and decisions were not superficial and hastily selected. Furthermore, since in the present instance the highly informed experts had extremely close agreement, there appears to be considerable justification for considering the standards set by them as *good*. Finally, unless a consensus of expert opinion is used to denote the good standard, there is no possibility of research with controversial social problems of a non-investigative type.

Still another limitation is the type of problem—experimental task—used in the study. The limitation is not in its failing to be a lifelike problem. It is rather that there are numerous other lifelike problems on which preconceived attitudes are undoubtedly more deeply ingrained with the probability that changes in attitude and choice of solution would occur much more slowly.

A more important limitation has reference to the way in which the information on the problem was presented. In actual life situations the individual normally has to sift the pertinent information from the impertinent, the facts from the propaganda and persuasion. Interpretation of fact is often presented as fact or indistinguishable from it. In the present research pertinent factual information only was presented.

Finally, one must avoid interpreting the results as the outgrowth of information alone or discussion alone. In the present study it is impossible to separate the effects of information alone from those of discussion alone. The results are the effects of available information compared with the effects of available information plus discussion.

Within these limitations the findings may certainly be given application. They may justifiably be applied to young adults considering similar social problems with procedure similar to that of this research.

CHAPTER III

THE EFFECT OF INFORMATION AND DISCUSSION ON RANKING SOLUTIONS TO A SOCIAL PROBLEM

INTRODUCTION

As HAS already been pointed out, in this study the interest centers primarily on the outcomes of discussion in terms of the participant's attitude and choice of solution. This chapter deals with the outcomes in terms of choice of solution. Inasmuch as the procedure with reference to ranking the solutions was essentially the same in the two experiments, the exposition of the results found in the two schools will be presented in parallel form so that comparisons can more readily be made and the findings of one experiment may add support to, or cast doubt on, the findings of the other.

It will be recalled that a score of zero on the Ranking Sheet indicated exact agreement with the experts' ranking of the five solutions and that any score was the sum of the squared deviations from the experts' ranking. Consequently, the larger the score the less closely the individual agreed with the experts whose ranking has been assumed to be the good answer.

GAINS IN RANKING SCORE FOR EXPERIMENTAL AND CONTROL STUDENTS

Table I summarizes the means, standard deviations, and standard errors of the means of the ranking scores made at each stage of the experiment. In this table and in all subsequent ones, unless otherwise noted, there were for Experiment A 265 experimental subjects and 69 control subjects, for Experiment B 194 experimental subjects and 144 control subjects. Examination of Table I reveals immediately that there was no significant difference between the experimental students and the control students with reference to the scores made on the first day before any of the

TABLE I

Summary of Means, Sigmas, and Standard Errors of Means for Each Day's Ranking Scores for Experimental and Control Subjects of Experiment A and Experiment B

Stage of Experiment	Experiment A						Experiment B						Experiment B, Paired SS					
	Experimental SS			Control SS			Experimental SS			Control SS			Experimental SS			Control SS		
	M	σ	σ_M	M	σ	σ_M	M	σ	σ_M	M	σ	σ_M	M	σ	σ_M	M	σ	σ_M
1st day.	20.25	7.08	0.43	21.25	5.08	0.71	17.00	7.71	0.55	17.61	8.44	0.70	16.99	7.72	0.68	17.17	8.32	0.73
2nd day.	9.00	10.08	0.61	9.84	11.27	1.37	4.72	7.20	0.52	6.79	9.84	0.83	4.90	7.54	0.66	4.90	7.54	0.66
3rd day.	3.31	6.70	0.41	6.46	8.50	1.02	1.71	3.82	0.29	4.85	8.76	0.73	1.83	4.03	0.35	3.91	7.87	0.69
4th day.	4.85	8.46	0.52	5.89	8.62	1.04	2.07	4.60	0.33	4.85	8.22	0.69	1.74	3.98	0.35	3.97	7.37	0.65

TABLE II

Summary of Means, Sigmas, and Standard Errors of Means for Changes in Ranking Scores at Each Stage of the Experiment for Experimental and Control Subjects of Experiment A and Experiment B

Stage of Experiment	Experiment A						Experiment B						Experiment B, Paired SS					
	Experimental SS			Control SS			Experimental SS			Control SS			Experimental SS			Control SS		
	M	σ	σ_M	M	σ	σ_M	M	σ	σ_M	M	σ	σ_M	M	σ	σ_M	M	σ	σ_M
Days 1-2.	11.25	11.41	0.70	11.42	11.78	1.42	12.28	10.30	0.74	10.82	12.42	1.04	12.09	10.50	0.92	12.27	10.60	0.93
Days 2-3.	5.70	8.72	0.54	3.36	8.36	1.01	3.00	5.83	0.42	1.94	8.11	0.68	3.08	5.64	0.49	0.98	6.03	0.53
Days 3-4.	-1.55	2.92	0.18	0.57	5.94	0.72	-0.36	4.22	0.30	0	5.18	0.43	0.09	2.68	0.24	-0.06	4.87	0.43

experimental factors had been introduced. This was true both in Experiment A and in Experiment B. The initial scores for the subjects in Experiment B were, however, better (lower) than were the initial scores in Experiment A. Experiment A scores represent approximately what one would expect from chance. Experiment B scores were slightly better than chance. It has already been noted that the general ability level of the students in Experiment B was higher than in Experiment A. The correlation between first day's ranking scores and general ability for the students in Experiment B was .15 with a PE$_r$ of .04. With such a low correlation it is hardly likely that this initial difference was due entirely to the low positive correlation. It was more probably due in part to a slightly greater average maturity on the part of the Experiment B subjects, a greater proportion of whom were seniors. It may be, too, that the students in Experiment B were somewhat more highly informed initially. It is, of course, possible that all three of these factors together accounted for the difference.

It may also be seen from Table I that the second day's scores for all students of both experiments were greatly superior to those of the first day. This improvement was of course due to the reading and study of the information pamphlet, to learning what the various systems mentioned in the alternatives really are. Why there should have been a difference in the gains made by the control students and the experimental students in Experiment B is not clear. The experimental procedures were exactly the same for both. Consequently, one can only hazard the guess that chance or some background factor unaccounted for was operating to cause one group to improve considerably more than the other.

On the third day all groups improved still more, the discussing experimental students more than the control students who restudied the information pamphlet. Whether the differences between the experimental students and the controls were significant will be considered later in this chapter when the changes in ranking scores are discussed.

On the fourth day, one month later, both experimental groups had a slight loss in score. Neither control group lost; one showed a slight gain. Apparently, the improvement in score was for the most part retained.

In Table II, the data presented in Table I have been treated somewhat differently. Instead of using raw gross scores, Table II presents means, sigmas, and standard errors of *changes* in ranking score made from the first to the second day—from the initial measurement to that taken immediately after reading; from the second day to the third day—from the measurement taken immediately after reading to that taken after the experimental subjects had discussed and the control subjects had restudied the information pamphlet; and from the third day to the fourth day—from that taken at the conclusion of the third day to that taken one month later. Examination of Table II reveals again the amount of gain made on the second and third days and the loss made by the experimental students between the third and fourth days. Judging from the size of the standard errors of the means in relation to the size of the means, one must conclude that most of the mean changes were highly reliable. The only ones which were not reliable are: the mean change for the control group of Experiment A from the third to the fourth days and the mean change for both the control and the experimental groups of Experiment B from the third to the fourth days. The fact that these changes from the third day to the fourth were unreliable is evidence that the rankings arrived at as a result of the reading and the discussion were on the whole well retained. It will be noted that the only group showing an improvement from the third to the fourth day was the Experiment A control group. This change was definitely unreliable.

We are, however, mainly interested in whether the discussing groups improved more than did those who did not discuss but who restudied the information pamphlet. The data in Table II show that the Experiment A experimental students had a mean gain of 5.70, while the Experiment A control students gained 3.36 between the measurement taken after reading and that taken after discussion or the restudy of the pamphlet. Was the difference in gains, 2.34 in favor of the discussing students, significant? Dividing the sigma of the difference into the obtained difference gives a critical ratio of 2.04. Interpreted, this indicates that there are about two chances in 100 that the true difference was zero or in favor of the control students. One cannot, then, be absolutely sure that the experimental students gained more from discussion than the control students did from restudy. One can, however, feel practically certain if the students of Experiment B show similar directional tendencies.

Did the students in Experiment B have a similar difference? Table II indicates a mean gain of 3.00 for the discussing students and a mean gain of 1.94 for those who restudied. The difference in favor of the discussing students was 1.06. Dividing the difference by the standard error of the difference gives a critical ratio of only 1.32, which interpreted means that there are about ten chances in 100 that the true difference was zero or in favor of the non-discussing students. Perhaps the reason Experiment B showed a less reliable difference in favor of the discussing students is that the experimental and control students were unequal in ranking score on the second day after reading. This can be seen from the data in Table I, and again in terms of changes in Table II. In order to check this point, 129 experimental students were paired with 129 control students on the basis of their second day's ranking scores. Then the mean ranking scores and the mean changes in ranking scores were computed. These computations are summarized in the right-hand columns of Tables I and II. The mean gain for the experimental students after discussion was 3.08, for the control students after restudy 0.98. The difference in favor of the discussing students was 2.10. The standard error of the difference was 0.72, the critical ratio 2.92. This indicates that there are only about two chances in 1000 that the true difference was zero or in favor of the restudying control students. Consequently, we can be fairly certain that this represented a real difference in favor of the discussing students. Since, moreover, it pointed even more strongly in the same direction than did the comparable results for Experiment A, we may be doubly certain that there was a real difference which favored the discussing students.

The matter of the results of one experiment adding to the reliability of the other when both show fairly large differences may be checked by combining the data from the two experiments. In this connection it should be recalled that the procedures in the two experiments varied slightly, as indicated in Chapter II. When the data were combined, the difference was 2.16 in favor of the discussing students. The sigma of the difference was 0.65 and the critical ratio was 3.32, a fact which indicated that a reliably larger gain was made by those who discussed as compared with those who restudied.

Did the individuals who studied and discussed retain their choices of solution as well as those who read and restudied? Referring again to Table II, we note that in Experiment A there was a difference of 2.12 favoring the control students, that the experimental students lost on the average 1.55 in ranking score while the controls gained 0.57 during the month following the experiment. The loss of the experimentals, however, it will be noted in Table I, was not sufficient to make the controls equal to the experimental students. Was this difference significant? The standard error of the difference divided into the difference gives a critical ratio of 2.86, which means that there is only about one chance in 100 that the real difference was zero or in favor of the experimental students.

Did the students in Experiment B show a similar difference between the third and fourth days? Table II indicates that the experimental students lost on the average —0.36 in ranking score between the end of the experiment and a date one month later. During the same period the control students made neither loss nor gain. The obtained difference was 0.36 in favor of the control students. The difference divided by the sigma of the difference gives a critical ratio of only 0.69. The difference was then unreliable. But again, because the control and the experimental students for some reason had unequal mean scores on the second day of the experiment, it is best to consider the data for the 129 experimental students and 129 control students paired on the basis of their second day's ranking scores. The difference was 0.15 in favor of the experimental students. The sigma of the difference was 0.49 and the critical ratio only 0.31. The difference then was very unreliable. We must conclude that the experimental students retained their ranking scores in Experiment B as well as did the control students.

When the data on retention of ranking scores from both experiments were combined, the difference was 1.27 favoring the controls. With the sigma of the difference of 0.57 and a critical ratio of 2.23, we must conclude that the retention differences were unreliable.

Summary. At this point the following conclusions appear justified:

1. As a result of the experimental procedures, both experimental and control students had better ranking scores at the end of the experiment than at the beginning.

2. After reading, both control and experimental students had reliable gains in ranking scores.

3. The experimental students had significant gains after discussion.

4. The control students had significant gains after restudy.

5. The changes made during the one-month interval were unreliable with one exception: The experimental students in Experiment A had a reliable loss.

6. Considering the data for the two experiments separately and together, the discussing students made a reliably larger mean gain after discussion than the control students after restudy.

7. The difference in retention of ranking score during the one-month interval was unreliable.

INDIVIDUAL GAINS ACCORDING TO TYPE OF DISCUSSION GROUP

It will be recalled that on the third day the experimental students were placed in discussion groups on the basis of their second day's ranking scores. Six types of groups, as indicated in Chapter II, were formed. With reference to these six group types, we are interested in the answers to such questions as the following: Did the individuals with good scores gain more in ranking score when discussing with other good students than when discussing with intermediate or poor students? What type of individual relative to the second day's ranking scores caused the intermediate students to improve most? Is it most advantageous for an initially poor individual to discuss with good, intermediate, or other poor students? Table III gives a summary of the data on gains in individual ranking scores after discussion for good, intermediate, and poor students who discussed with good, intermediate, and poor students. (It should again be emphasized that *good, intermediate,* and *poor* do not refer to the individual's ability but to his second day's ranking score.) It will be noted in this table that the data of Experiment B were combined with those of Experiment A in the right-hand columns. The data of Experiment B are not presented separately because of the small number of cases in many of the rows. This is due to the fact that the scores in Experiment B were considerably higher, with the result that there were many fewer intermediate and poor students when the same standards were used as in Experiment A.

Considering the data in Table III for the students of Experiment A alone and of Experiments A and B combined, we note that all groups except the good who discussed with poor made at least a slight gain. The gains were uneven: the good students gained relatively little; the intermediate students a great deal; and the poor students a still larger amount. The unevenness of the

TABLE III

Summary of Data on Gains in Individual Ranking Scores after Discussion for Good, Intermediate, and Poor Experimental Subjects, Experiment A and Experiments A and B Combined

Type of Individual	Discussing with:	EXPERIMENT A				EXPERIMENTS A AND B COMBINED			
		N	M gain	σ	σ_M	N	M gain	σ	σ_M
Good	Good	52	0.49	1.70	0.22	159	0.55	1.09	0.09
Good	Intermediate	36	0.11	1.41	0.24	50	0.04	0.65	0.09
Good	Poor	25	0	0.80	0.16	32	−0.69	1.08	0.19
Intermediate	Good	36	5.87	2.86	0.48	49	6.16	3.12	0.45
Intermediate	Intermediate	24	5.42	4.46	0.91	43	5.30	3.94	0.60
Intermediate	Poor	21	2.29	7.20	1.57	34	3.24	6.29	1.08
Poor	Good	25	19.28	7.72	1.54	32	18.63	7.70	1.36
Poor	Intermediate	21	16.19	11.38	2.48	31	16.52	10.20	1.83
Poor	Poor	28	9.71	10.18	1.92	32	8.81	10.10	1.78

gains for the three different types of individuals (good, intermediate, and poor) was undoubtedly due largely to the differences in the amount each could gain. In Experiment A, for example, only eight of the thirty-six good individuals who discussed with intermediates could gain; the others already had perfect scores. Only four of the twenty-five good individuals who discussed with poor individuals could possibly gain. In order to be sure of some basis for discussion, in the forming of the groups an effort was made to place some individuals who could gain in the Type I groups (good discussing with good). As a result the good students who discussed with intermediates and poor students generally had perfect scores before discussion. In view of this fact data on the good individuals can be dismissed with little more than a glance, except to note that those individuals who could gain generally did gain. Because of the large differences in the amount each of the three types could gain, it will be well to confine comparisons to the individuals of one type who discussed with each of the other types rather than to attempt any comparisons between such items as *good discussing with good* and *poor discussing with poor,* which are obviously not subject to reasonable comparison.

If the mean gain in each case is divided by the standard error of that mean, the number of sigmas to the zero point is obtained. This gives an index of reliability for each gain. The results of such divisions are given below:

Types of Individuals Discussing	*Number of Sigmas to the Zero Point:*	
	Experiment A	*Experiments* A *and* B *Combined*
Good with good	2.23	6.11
Good with intermediate	0.46	0.44
Good with poor	0	3.63
Intermediate with good	12.04	13.44
Intermediate with intermediate	5.95	8.83
Intermediate with poor	1.46	3.00
Poor with good	12.52	13.69
Poor with intermediate	6.53	9.03
Poor with poor	5.06	4.95

One can be practically certain that a gain is reliable if the zero point is at least three sigmas away from the mean gain. For Experiment A, omitting the good discussing with good, intermediate, and poor individuals, one notes that most of the gains were such as to make one practically certain that they were reliable. The exception (in addition to the good with good, intermediate, and poor) is the intermediates after discussing with the poor. The lack of statistical reliability in this case was probably due to the small number of cases. For when Experiments A and B were combined, there was very little increase in the mean gain, as shown in Table III. At the same time there was for the intermediates discussing with the poor an increase from 1.46 to 3.00 sigmas to the zero point. Consequently, when the students of Experiments A and B were combined, we may be practically certain that the intermediate and the poor students made gains regardless of with whom they discussed.

It is striking that with the exception of when the good discussed with the poor (and then only slightly) the good individuals were not pulled down when discussing with other types. Whether more than an averaging process was taking place one cannot be certain. The fact that good students were pulled down very little, if at all, was probably due in part to the greater confidence with which they held their opinions. Thorndike [32, p. 255] has shown that individual confidence is a factor in determining the group answer.

It is also striking that the poor gained a great deal even when discussing with other equally poor individuals, not so much of course as when they discussed with intermediate or good students. The gain of the poor discussing with poor was probably in part due to the tendency for discussion to cancel out one another's errors. A part of it may have been due to more inherent values in discussion, the criticism and evaluation of one another's suggestions and the larger number of suggestions made.

Let us now turn to comparisons between the amounts gained by a type of individual after discussing with others of the same type or with the other two types. Were the differences significant? Table IV summarizes the data on this point. If the difference divided by the sigma of the difference gives a critical ratio of three or more, we can be practically certain of a real difference. In the column giving the critical ratios for Experiment A we see only one ratio of three or more. That one is for the poor with good compared with the poor with poor. This single reliable difference indicates that the poor did significantly better when discussing with good individuals than when discussing with other poor students. Other differences would probably have been reli-

TABLE IV

*Differences in Mean Ranking Score Gains after Discussion
for Good, Intermediate, and Poor Students Evaluated in
Terms of the Standard Errors of Those Differences,
Experiment A and Experiments A and B Combined*

M minus M	EXPERIMENT A			EXPERIMENTS A AND B COMBINED		
	Diff.	σdiff.	d / σdiff.	Diff.	σdiff.	d / σdiff.
Good-good minus good-interm.......	0.38	0.33	1.15	0.51	0.13	4.33
Good-interm. minus good-poor......	0.11	0.29	0.38	0.73	0.21	3.48
Good-good minus good-poor........	0.49	0.27	1.82	1.24	0.21	5.91
Interm.-good minus interm.-interm...	0.36	1.03	0.35	0.86	0.75	1.15
Interm.-interm. minus interm.-poor..	3.13	1.81	1.73	2.06	1.23	1.67
Interm.-good minus interm.-poor....	3.49	1.64	2.15	2.92	1.17	2.50
Poor-good minus poor-interm........	3.09	2.92	1.06	2.11	2.28	0.93
Poor-interm. minus poor-poor.......	6.48	3.14	2.06	7.71	2.55	3.02
Poor-good minus poor-poor.........	9.57	2.46	3.89	9.82	2.24	4.38

able if the number of cases had been larger. When, therefore, the data on these points for both Experiments A and B were combined, other significant differences were found. Good individuals discussing with other good individuals had significantly larger gains than good individuals discussing with intermediate. And good individuals discussing with intermediate individuals had significantly larger gains than good students discussing with poor, but not so significant a gain as did the good with good compared with the good with poor.

Of the intermediate students those who discussed with good

had larger gains than did intermediates with intermediates, and the intermediates with intermediates had larger gains than the intermediates with poor. The intermediates with good gained more than the intermediates with poor. The differences, however, were not such as to cause us to be certain. Of the comparisons involving poor students discussing with others the poor with intermediate made significantly larger gains than did the poor with poor, and the poor with good than the poor with poor. The poor with good, however, did not show significantly larger gains than did the poor with intermediate.

It is worthy of note that the trend throughout all of these differences was identical. Even though some of the differences were not reliable, the similarity of trend gives corroborating evidence that the greatest improvement occurred when good individuals were included in the group, that the next greatest improvement occurred when intermediate students were included, and that the least improvement resulted when the poor were included.

The differences in gains for the three types of individuals discussing with the three types were also considered by the statistical method known as analysis of variance. This method is described in detail in Snedecor's *Statistical Methods* [26]. With this method one may treat several groups at once, learning whether the variation among their means is greater than is consistent with the hypothesis that they are all random samples of the same population. Above we noted the trend that the better the companion the more the improvement in ranking score following discussion. Analysis of variance for the data for Experiments A and B combined (Table III) will make it possible to determine more accurately whether the trend was more than a matter of chance.

Table V gives the analysis of variance for the data on gains in individual ranking scores after discussion for good, intermediate, and poor subjects who discussed with good, intermediate, and poor subjects. The values in the F_{05} and F_{01} columns are from Snedecor's table interpreting F's. The F_{05} value indicates that random sampling alone might produce an F as large as this or larger in 5 per cent of all random samples from the population. The F_{01} is one that might be expected in 1 per cent of the

random samples from the population. The F values in Table V
are in all three cases much larger than the F_{01} and F_{05} values.
Interpreted, this means that the F values are reliable. It is very
unlikely that they are due to accidents of sampling. The F of
26.36 for variation among types of companions indicates that
the mean changes between groups were too great to be attributed
to sampling errors. The type of companion with whom an individual discussed almost certainly made a difference in the amount of
ranking score gain. This is the same as saying, as above, that the

TABLE V

*Analysis of Variance for Individual Gains in Ranking
Scores Made by Three Types of Individuals after
Discussing with Three Types of Individuals*

Source of Variation	Sum of Squares	Degrees of Freedom	Mean Square	F	F_{05}	F_{01}
Among types of companion	1280.88	2	640.44	26.36	3.02	4.66
Among initial perform-ance levels..............	14068.27	2	7034.14	289.47	3.02	4.66
Interaction..............	664.48	4	166.12	6.84	2.39	3.36
Among individuals in the same category (error variance)........	11000.98	453	24.30			
Total..............	27014.61	461				

better the type of companion in discussion, the greater the improvement in ranking score. The F of 289.47 for variation among
performance levels (good, intermediate, and poor levels before
discussion) indicates that the level of initial score almost certainly
influenced the amount of gain. This bears out the earlier rather
obvious observation that the gains were uneven, the good gaining
least, the intermediate an intermediate amount, and the poor the
most. This unevenness as determined by the gain in ranking was
primarily a function of the amount each type could gain, the poor
having much opportunity to gain and the good having very little
opportunity. The F of 6.84 for interaction between types of companion and performance levels indicates that not all types of
initial performance level reacted in the same way to different
types of companion. In other words, initially poor individuals

gained more when discussing with good individuals than when discussing with poor; the type of companion meant less to the initially good.

These findings, then, confirm the findings indicated earlier for differences in mean changes in ranking score for the three types of individuals discussing with the three types.

In part we seem here to be corroborating Simpson's finding that the most able exert more influence than the less able in discussion [25, pp. 53-54]. For here the greatest improvement occurred when the discussions were with good individuals. In this connection it may be well to note a fact which will be mentioned again later; namely, the correlation between general ability and good ranking score after reading was only .28 in Experiment A and .26 in Experiment B. Simpson's correlation was also low. Consequently, the high in general ability were not always the good.

Summary. The following conclusions may be made for the section just completed:

1. All types of students (good, intermediate, and poor with respect to ranking score after reading) had mean gains in ranking the solutions after discussion. The one exception was the good who discussed with poor when the data for Experiments A and B were combined. The gains were largest for the poor, smaller for the intermediate, and smallest for the good. The unevenness of gain was probably largely due to the differing amounts each could gain. Practically all of the gains were reliable or near reliable.

2. Good individuals were pulled down not at all or very little after discussing with poor individuals, and poor individuals made highly reliable gains in ranking the solutions after discussing with equally poor students.

3. Good individuals after discussing with other good individuals made significantly larger gains than good individuals after discussing with poor. Good individuals after discussing with intermediate had significantly larger gains than the good after discussing with poor, but not so significant a gain as the good with good had over the good with poor.

4. The intermediate after discussing with good gained more

than did the intermediates after discussing with poor. The intermediates discussing with intermediates gained more than did the intermediates with poor. The intermediates with good gained more than did the intermediates with intermediates. None of these differences was reliable.

5. The poor with good did not gain significantly more than the poor who discussed with intermediates. The poor who discussed with intermediates and the poor who discussed with good did gain significantly more than the poor who discussed with poor.

6. The trend of a group being best when any type discussed with good, next best when it discussed with intermediate, and third best when it discussed with poor, is worthy of note and tends to make even the unreliable differences appear more important. Analysis of variance showed this trend to have been reliable.

INDIVIDUAL GAINS IN RANKING SCORE FOR TWO ABILITY GROUPS

We have seen that there were differences in the gains made by the individuals differing in ranking score before discussion. Did different ability groups gain similarly or differently? Were there differences between those who discussed and those who restudied while the others were discussing? The answers to these questions are found in the data summarized in Tables VI and VII. Two ability groups chosen on the basis of the students' raw scores on the Ohio State University Psychological Test, Form 20, were considered. These two groups were termed the low-ability group and the high-ability group. Each contained about 30 per cent of the students. The low-ability group had raw scores ranging from 10 to 39. The scores for the high-ability group ranged from 70 to 150. These segments were used so that ability differences might be detected more readily. Inasmuch as the average ability score for the students in Experiment A was about 55 and for those in Experiment B about 60, these two groups included the students in the upper and lower segments of general ability for the populations considered.

The data of Tables VIA and VIB indicate that the low-ability groups, both experimental and control, in both Experiment

TABLE VIA

Summary of Data on Gains in Ranking Score from Reading
*for Two Ability Groups of the Experimental
and Control Subjects*

Ability Group	Experiment A				Experiment B				Experiments A and B Combined			
	N	M	σ	σ_M	N	M	σ	σ_M	N	M	σ	σ_M
Low experimental....	81	8.94	12.06	1.32	51	10.86	11.82	1.66	132	9.62	12.26	1.07
High experimental....	59	13.61	10.40	1.32	73	12.79	9.60	1.33	132	13.26	9.89	0.86
Low control.	26	11.33	11.24	2.20	37	10.27	11.58	1.90	63	10.41	11.91	1.50
High control	16	15.25	10.98	2.75	47	11.66	11.48	1.67	63	12.57	10.88	1.38
Low control and low experimental combined...									195	9.88	12.04	0.86
High control and high experimental combined...									195	13.03	10.18	0.73

TABLE VIB

*Summary of Data on Gains in Ranking Score for Two Ability
Groups, the Experimental Subjects from* Discussing
and the Control Subjects from Restudying

Ability Group	Experiment A				Experiment B				Experiments A and B Combined			
	N	M	σ	σ_M	N	M	σ	σ_M	N	M	σ	σ_M
Low experimental....	81	8.42	9.43	1.04	51	4.62	7.44	1.04	132	7.15	8.80	0.77
High experimental....	59	3.46	6.44	0.84	73	1.75	4.60	0.54	132	2.51	5.56	0.49
Low control..	26	3.31	8.82	1.73	37	2.32	8.58	1.25	63	2.73	8.70	1.10
High control.	16	0.63	3.50	0.88	47	1.23	3.16	0.44	63	1.08	3.17	0.40

A and Experiment B gained less from reading than did the high-ability groups. The low-ability groups, however, gained more from discussion or restudy than did the high-ability groups. This was true in both experiments for both experimental and control students. A comparison of the size of the standard errors with the size of the mean gains shows that in all but four instances the mean gains were well over three times as large as their standard errors. Interpreted, this means that in all cases but four the gains were significant, that is, statistically reliable. The gains were not statistically reliable for the high- and the low-ability control students of Experiment A after restudying the information pamphlet or for the low- and the high-ability control students of Experiment B after restudying the information pamphlet.

It appears, then, that the gains from reading were statistically reliable for all students both high and low for both experiments. The gains made after subsequent discussion were statistically reliable for all discussing students both high and low in ability for both experiments. The gains made by the low- and the high-ability control students from restudy were unreliable.

Another question now presents itself: Were the differences in gains made by the different ability groups statistically significant? The question may be answered by referring to Table VII, which gives the critical ratios for several comparisons. It will be noted at once that the critical ratios for the comparisons for Experiment A were considerably larger than those for Experiment B. The differences were, however, in every case in the same direction. Those for Experiment B would undoubtedly have been larger had it not been that the students in Experiment B had less opportunity to gain from the discussion. Another factor lowering the differences in Experiment B may possibly have been the extra emphasis placed on restudy with the control students in that experiment. Table VII also gives the critical ratios for the comparisons with the data from the two experiments combined.

Did the high-ability control students gain more from the first reading than the low-ability control students? Although the differences in both Experiment A and Experiment B were in favor of the high-ability control students, in neither case was the critical ratio indicative of a significant difference. The high-ability experimental students of Experiments A and B gained more from reading than did the low-ability experimental students. Again, in neither experiment was the critical ratio large enough for statistical significance. When the data from both experiments were

TABLE VII

Differences in Mean Gains in Ranking Score for Two Ability Groups of the Experimental and Control Subjects Evaluated in Terms of the Standard Errors of Those Differences

M minus M	EXPERIMENT A			EXPERIMENT B			EXPERIMENTS A AND B COMBINED		
	d	σd	d/σd	d	σd	d/σd	d	σd	d/σd
Low control minus high control, reading......	-4.22	3.52	1.20	-1.39	2.53	0.55	-2.16	2.04	1.06
Low experimental minus high experimental, reading.............	-4.67	1.87	2.50	-1.93	2.13	0.91	-3.64	1.37	2.66
Low control and experimental minus high control and experimental, reading							-3.15	1.13	2.79
Low control minus high control, restudy......	2.68	1.94	1.38	1.09	1.32	0.83	1.65	1.17	1.41
Low experimental minus high experimental, discussing.............	4.96	1.34	3.70	2.87	1.17	2.45	4.64	0.91	5.10
Low experimental, discussing minus low control, restudy.........	5.11	2.02	2.53	2.30	1.63	1.41	4.42	1.34	3.30
High experimental, discussing minus high control, restudy......	2.83	1.22	2.32	0.52	0.71	0.73	1.43	0.63	2.27

combined, the differences remained definitely unreliable. When the data for experimental and control students for both experiments were combined, the difference in gains from reading made by the high-ability students over the low-ability students closely approached reliability. The critical ratio was 2.79, indicating less than one chance in 100 that the true difference was zero or in favor of the low-ability students. Consequently, we may conclude with considerable assurance that the high-ability students, experimental and control, did gain significantly more than the low-ability students from the first reading of the information pamphlet.

Did the low-ability control students gain more from the restudy on the third day than the high-ability control students? The critical ratio for the difference in Experiment A was 1.38, for

Experiment B 0.83, both in favor of the low-ability control students. In neither case was the size of the ratio indicative of reliability. When the data for both experiments were combined, the difference remained unreliable, having a critical ratio of only 1.41. Consequently, there was no significant difference in the gains of the high- and the low-ability control students after restudy.

Did the low-ability experimental students gain more from discussing than the high-ability experimental students? In both Experiment A and Experiment B the difference was in favor of the low-ability experimental students. In the former the critical ratio was 3.70 and in the latter 2.45. The first ratio indicates statistical significance; the second closely approaches significance. When the data for both experiments were combined, the critical ratio became 5.10, indicating a definitely reliable difference. Therefore, we may conclude with assurance that the low-ability experimental students profited more from discussion than the high-ability experimental students. Inasmuch as later in this chapter the correlation between ability and good ranking score is shown to have been very low, it is probable that the difference was the result of the discussion rather than the amount each could gain. The opinions of the low-ability group were probably less fixed and more subject to change.

From the point of view of the purpose of this study still more interesting differences were those between the gains made by low- and high-ability students from discussion and those made by similar students from restudy on the third day of the procedure. Two questions are in order. Did the low-ability experimental students gain more or less from discussion than did the low-ability control students from restudy? And did the high-ability experimental students gain more or less from discussion than did the high-ability control students from restudy? The low-ability groups in both experiments gained more from discussion than the low-ability groups did from the individual restudy of the information pamphlet. For Experiment A the critical ratio was 2.53, for Experiment B 1.41. The latter ratio, interpreted, indicates that there are about eight chances in 100 that the true difference was zero or in favor of the students who restudied. The former indicates that there is about one chance in 100 that the true difference was zero or in favor of the control students. When the data from both experiments were combined, the difference in favor of the low-ability experimental students had a critical ratio of 3.30. Therefore, we may conclude with assurance that the low-ability discussing students gained more from discussing than the low-ability students did from restudying.

When the high-ability students are considered, we find similar results. Those who discussed gained more than those who restudied the information pamphlet. In Experiment A the difference in favor of the discussing students had a critical ratio of 2.32; in Experiment B the ratio was again lower, being 0.73. The first ratio indicates there are about two chances in 100, the latter about twenty-three chances in 100, that the true difference was zero or in favor of the non-discussing students. The data for both experiments combined gave a critical ratio of 2.27 in favor of the high-ability experimental students. We cannot then conclude with assurance that the high-ability discussing students gained significantly more than the high-ability restudying students.

Summary. The following conclusions to this section of the chapter appear justified:

1. After reading both high- and low-ability experimental and control groups made reliable gains in ranking scores.

2. After subsequent discussion both high- and low-ability experimental students had reliable gains in ranking scores.

3. After restudy both high- and low-ability control groups made gains, none of which was reliable.

4. The high-ability students gained more in ranking score from the first reading than did the low-ability students. The difference closely approached reliability.

5. The low-ability control students gained unreliably more from the restudy than did the high-ability control students. The low-ability experimental students gained significantly more in ranking score after discussion than did the high-ability experimental students.

6. The low-ability discussing students gained reliably more from discussing than did the low-ability students from restudying.

7. The high-ability students gained unreliably more in ranking score from discussion than did the high-ability control students from restudy.

ADDITIONAL CONSIDERATIONS WITH REFERENCE TO RANKING SCORES

It will be recalled from Chapter II that the discussion groups presented group reports which included a group ranking of the five solutions to the parole problem. Inasmuch as this study is concerned with the effect of discussion on the individual and inasmuch as it is felt that the individual ranking made after the completion of the group report tells more accurately the effect on the individual, no use has been made of the group ranking scores. It may be interesting, however, to consider briefly to what extent the group scores corresponded with those of the individuals comprising the group. It is possible, of course, that some individuals merely went along with the group in order to avoid argument while at the same time reserving their own opinions to themselves. In order to learn the extent to which the individuals were really influenced by the discussion, the correlation between group ranking score after discussion and individual ranking score after discussion was computed. The r was .82, the PE_r .01. To a large extent, then, the group decisions became the opinions of the individual members of the group. In connection with this topic it may be interesting to consider whether the group ranking scores were significantly better than the individual ranking scores. After discussion 71 groups had a mean ranking score of 2.93. The standard deviation was 6.02 and the standard error of the mean 0.72. The 265 subjects who discussed in these groups had, after discussion, a mean ranking score of 3.31 with a standard deviation of 6.70 and a standard error of the mean of 0.41. The difference of 0.38 favoring the groups had a standard error of the difference equaling 0.83. The critical ratio, then, was only 0.46, indicative of unreliability. The group scores after discussion thus were not significantly better than the individual scores after discussion. In the computations earlier in this chapter which treated of differences between the experimental and the control students the individual ranking scores were used in every instance. The fact that one month after the close of the experiment (see Table I) the experimental students still had ranking scores better on the average than those of the control students is additional evidence that the effects of the discussion were relatively permanent, in spite of the fact that the discussing students lost more during the interval than the non-discussing students.

A few additional correlations may shed some light on the data already presented. In part these have been referred to earlier in this chapter. Correlations were computed for the relationship between ability as measured by the Ohio State University Psychological Test, Form 20 and good ranking score. The correlation between ability and good initial ranking score was .05 with a PE_r of .04 for the students of Experiment A, 15 ± .04 for the students of Experiment B. That for ability and good ranking score after reading (experimental and control students combined) was .28 ± .03 for Experiment A, .26 ± .03 for Experiment B. The correlation for the experimental students only after discussing on the third day was .13 ± .04 in Experiment A and .19 ± .15 in Experiment B. The correlation for the control students only after restudying on the third day was .24 ± .01 in Experiment A and .17 ± .06 in Experiment B. Not all of these correlations were reliable, inasmuch as for reliability the correlation should be at least four times its probable error. All show a slight correlation between high ability score and good ranking score, but that is about all that can be said for them. The r's (all computed by the Pearson product-moment method) probably would have shown closer relationships after reading, discussion, and restudy had not a large number of the students had perfect scores.

Furthermore, the critical ratio of the differences between the experimental and the control students, the discussing and the restudying students, was so small as to be highly unreliable. In Experiment A the difference in correlation was .11, the control students showing a closer relationship between ability score and good ranking score at the end of the third day. The probable error of the difference, however, was .09, giving a critical ratio of only 1.22. There are only seventy-nine chances in 100 that this difference represented a true difference. In Experiment B the difference and the resulting critical ratio were even smaller.

We must conclude, then, that for the populations, the materials, and the procedures used there was little relationship between ability as measured by the test used and choice of solution.

SUMMARY

Since each section of the chapter has its own summary, it is unnecessary to summarize in detail the findings of the experiments with reference to individual ranking scores. The following rather general conclusions, however, may be made:

1. Both the students who read and discussed and those who read and restudied made reliable gains in ability to rank the given solutions to the social problem. The discussing students gained reliably more after discussion than the control students after restudy.

2. All types of subjects—good, intermediate, and poor with respect to ranking score after reading—gained in ranking score regardless of the type of student with whom they discussed. Good students were seldom pulled down after discussing with poor students. Poor students gained even after discussing with their fellows. Good students improved more after discussing with other good students than after discussing with intermediate or poor students. The intermediate students gained more after discussing with the good students than after discussing with other intermediates or with poor students. Poor students gained more after discussing with good students than after discussing with intermediates or with other poor students. While not all the differences were reliable, analysis of variance proved the existence of a trend for the largest improvement to accompany discussion with the companions having the best ranking scores before discussion.

3. Both high- and low-ability groups, experimental and control, made reliable gains in ranking score after reading. Both high- and low-ability experimental students made reliable gains after

discussion. Neither ability group made a reliable gain after restudy. The high-ability students gained more from reading than the low-ability students, the difference closely approaching reliability. The low-ability experimentals gained significantly more from the discussion than the high-ability experimental students. Low-ability students gained reliably more from discussion than low-ability students from restudy. Other differences were unreliable.

4. There was a low positive correlation between general ability score and ranking score, highest after reading. There was no significant difference between the r for control students and that for experimental students.

CHAPTER IV

THE EFFECT OF INFORMATION AND DISCUSSION ON ATTITUDE

In ADDITION to being interested in the cumulative effect of information and discussion on the individual's choice of solutions to a social problem, we are interested in the effect on his attitude. The answers to such questions as the following will help to determine the effect of information and discussion on attitude: When information alone was available were there changes in the direction of the appropriate attitude toward the social problem? Were there additional changes in the direction of the good attitude after discussion of the problem? Were there additional changes in the direction of the good attitude when students restudied the information instead of discussing? Did those who studied and restudied differ significantly in attitude from those who both studied and discussed? Did the individuals who studied and discussed retain their attitudes as well as those who studied and restudied?

It will be recalled that measures of attitude were different for the two experiments. Consequently, rather than discussing both in parallel, in this chapter the attitude data first for Experiment A and then for Experiment B will be considered. At the end of the chapter the findings of the two measures will be compared.

The attitude measure in Experiment A, as was pointed out in Chapter II, was the Remmers-Kelley generalized "Scale for Measuring Attitude toward Any Institution." The good attitude was assumed to be the average of the eleven scores secured from nine highly informed experts. This average score of 9.3 was given a value of zero. Students' attitude scores, then, were zero or plus or minus this point. The measure of attitude was taken four times: (1) at the beginning of the experiment, (2) after reading the information pamphlet, (3) after discussion or restudy, and (4) after an interval of one month.

I. Experiment A

GAINS IN ATTITUDE SCORE

Table VIII summarizes the essential data with reference to the attitude scores of the students in Experiment A. The raw data upon which the means, sigmas, and standard errors of the means were based were all in terms of positive or negative deviations from the standard set by the experts. The number of students is the same throughout the table, 265 experimental subjects and 69 control subjects. At the start of the experiment, before the presentation of any experimental materials, both the experimental and the control subjects had mean attitudes significantly less favorable to parole than the experts. The mean in each case was larger than three times its standard error. After reading the mean of both the experimental and the control students approached closely the standard held by experts. After discussion the mean of the experimental students fell away slightly, whereas that of the controls after restudy approached slightly closer to the experts' norm.

TABLE VIII

Summary of Means, Sigmas, and Standard Errors of Means for Each Day's Attitude Scores in Experiment A

Stage of Experiment	EXPERIMENTAL SS			CONTROL SS		
	M	σ	σ_M	M	σ	σ_M
1st day	−1.14	2.41	0.15	−1.22	2.51	0.30
2nd day	0.04	1.46	0.09	−0.26	1.95	0.24
3rd day	0.14	1.40	0.08	−0.19	1.70	0.20
4th day	−0.21	1.83	0.11	−0.30	1.76	0.21

After the month's interval the mean attitude of both the experimental and the control students moved slightly away from the experts' norm.

In Table IX the means, sigmas, and standard errors of means are for *changes* in attitude scores made from the beginning of the experiment to the measure after reading, from after reading to after discussion (or restudy), from after discussion (or restudy) to one month later. Examination of Table IX reveals again the fairly large gain made after reading by both the experimental and the control students, the slight or zero changes made by both after discussion or restudy and after the one-month interval. The discrepancies between Tables VIII and IX, in which, for example, the former shows a loss for the experimental students between the second and third days, whereas the latter shows a slight gain for this period, may be explained as follows: In Table VIII *scores* were tabulated with regard to the direction of their deviation from the norm. In Table IX *changes* in scores were tabulated with regard to the extent of the deviation from the norm and without regard to the direction of that deviation. For example, if the second score was positive the norm to the same degree as the first was negative, the shift was zero, and the computation for Table IX showed no change with

TABLE IX

Summary of Means, Sigmas, and Standard Errors of Means for Changes in Attitude Score at Each Stage of Experiment A

Stage of Experiment	Experimental SS			Control SS		
	M	σ	σ_M	M	σ	σ_M
Days 1-2 (after reading)....	0.94	2.12	0.13	0.81	1.81	0.22
Days 2-3 (after discussion or restudy).......	0.06	0.95	0.06	0.13	1.13	0.14
Days 3-4 (after one-month interval).......	−0.25	1.29	0.08	0	0.98	0.12

reference to the experts' standard. In Table VIII such a change in score would have moved the mean toward or beyond the experts' norm.

How many of these changes in attitude as represented by scores on the Remmers-Kelley scale in relation to the experts' standard were reliable? If the mean change divided by the standard error of the mean gives a figure of three or larger, we may be practically certain that the change was reliable. Only three such means were sufficiently large in relation to their standard errors to meet this criterion of reliability. The gains made after reading by both the experimental students and the control students were highly reliable. The critical ratio for the experimental students was 7.23, that for the control students 3.69. After discussing, however, the experimental students had a mean gain of only 0.06 with a standard error of the mean of 0.06. The critical ratio of 1.00 is unreliable. The control students had a mean gain after restudy of 0.13. But this mean had a standard error of 0.14, larger than the mean. The critical ratio was less than one, and consequently unreliable. After a month's interval the experimental students lost on the average 0.25. With a standard error of the mean of 0.08 the critical ratio exceeded three. The loss was consequently reliable. During the month's interval the control students on the average neither gained nor lost. This mean change of zero had a standard error of 0.11, indicative of unreliability.

About the only conclusion we can draw from the data summarized in Tables VIII and IX is that there was a definitely reliable gain in mean attitude after reading the information pamphlet on the second day. On subsequent days there were slight changes all except one of which may well have been due to chance. That one was the loss incurred by the experimental students during the month following the experiment.

Inasmuch as the mean changes in attitude (except for that following reading) were for the most part unreliable, we may well infer that the difference between the change made by the students who discussed and that made by those who restudied the information pamphlet was also unreliable. The inference is true. The difference was only 0.07, and although it was rather surprisingly in favor of the control students, the sigma of the difference was 0.15 and the critical ratio only 0.46. Consequently, for all practical purposes there was no difference in the gains made from discussion and from restudy.

The difference between the changes in attitude score relative to the experts' standard after the interval of one month was 0.25 in favor of the control students. All of this difference represented the loss made by the experimental students. The sigma of this difference was 0.14, the critical ratio 1.79. Consequently, the difference was unreliable.

Summary. We must then conclude that on the basis of the Remmers-Kelley scale there were no significant differences between the students who read about and discussed the problem and those who read about and restudied the problem.

GAINS IN ATTITUDE SCORE FOR TWO ABILITY GROUPS

Did the Remmers-Kelley scale show reliable differences between two ability groups, as measured by the Ohio State University Psychological Test, Form 20? The ability groups are of the same composition as in Chapter III. Tables X and XI summarize the data on gains in attitude score from reading and discussing for the low- and high-ability students. By comparing the size of the standard error of each mean with the mean, one can readily see which groups made significant gains. The results for the two ability groups are similar to those found for the groups without regard to ability. The experimental students of low ability

TABLE X

Summary of Data on Gains in Attitude Score from Reading for Two Ability Groups of the Experimental and Control Subjects, Experiment A Only

Ability Group	N	M	σ	σ_M
Low experimental	81	0.71	2.04	0.22
High experimental	59	1.21	2.16	0.27
Low control	26	0.77	1.67	0.33
High control	16	1.13	3.22	0.81

TABLE XI

Summary of Data on Gains in Attitude Score for Two Ability Groups, the Experimental Subjects from Discussing and the Control Subjects from Restudying, Experiment A Only

Ability Group	N	M	σ	σ_M
Low experimental	81	0.11	1.23	0.14
High experimental	59	0.07	0.77	0.10
Low control	26	0.31	1.85	0.36
High control	16	0.31	0.98	0.25

made a reliable gain from reading. The control students of low ability had a gain from reading that verges on reliability. The high-ability experimental students also made a reliable gain from reading. The high-ability control students did not show a reliable gain from reading, but this was probably due to the small number of cases which greatly increased the size of the standard error of the mean. The gains for neither ability group from discussing were reliable, the standard errors in each case being larger than the mean gains. The gains made by the control students after restudy of the information pamphlet were also unreliable. The standard error of the mean for the low-ability control group was larger than the mean gain, and the standard error of the mean for the high-ability group was only slightly smaller than the mean gain.

Were there reliable differences in the gains of the ability groups, control and experimental? The data showing evaluated differences in gains in attitude scores made by the two ability groups of the experimental and control students are presented in Table XII. The column indicating critical ratios shows no reliable differences.

Summary. Once again we conclude that for the parole problem and for the population considered there were no significant dif-

TABLE XII

Differences in Mean Attitude Score Gain for Two Ability Groups of the Experimental and Control Subjects Evaluated in Terms of the Standard Errors of Those Differences for Experiment A Only

M minus M	d	σd	$d/\sigma d$
Low control from reading minus high control from reading.	−0.56	0.87	0.64
Low control from restudy minus high control from restudy.	0	0.45	0
Low experimental from discussing minus low control from restudy.	−0.20	0.38	0.53
High experimental from discussing minus high control from restudy.	−0.24	0.27	0.89
Low experimental from reading minus high experimental from reading.	−0.50	0.35	1.43
Low experimental from discussing minus high experimental from discussing.	0.04	0.17	0.24

ferences in attitude gains, as measured by the Remmers-Kelley scale, between those who discussed and those who restudied. With the problem considered and with the population included the scale showed significant changes after reading and at no other time.

CORRELATIONS BETWEEN ABILITY SCORES AND ATTITUDE SCORES

The question may well be asked: Was there any correlation between ability as measured by the Ohio State University Psychological Test, Form 20 and goodness (with reference to the experts' standard) of attitude? The correlation between ability and goodness of attitude score at the beginning of the experiment before either reading or discussing occurred was —.04 with a PE$_r$ of .04. This was for the experimental and control groups combined. After reading the correlation for all subjects, control and experimental, was .04, the PE$_r$ .04. After discussion for the experimental subjects only the correlation was .04, the PE$_r$ .04. After a restudy of the information pamphlet the control subjects had a correlation of .02 with a PE$_r$ of .08. The probable errors in every case were as large as the correlations or larger. And since for reliability the correlation should be at least four times its probable error, no one of the correlations was reliable. Furthermore, the critical ratio of the difference between the subjects who discussed and those who restudied was so small that no real difference was indicated. The obtained difference in correlations after discussion and after restudy was .022, the experimental students having a correlation between general ability and goodness of attitude negligibly higher than that of the controls. As might be expected, the probable error of the difference was larger than the difference, being .089. The critical ratio was only 0.25. Interpreted, this means that there are only fifty-seven chances in 100 of a real difference. The r's (all computed by the Pearson product-moment method) might have been higher after reading, discussion, and restudy had not a large number of students had scores closely approximating the experts' norm.

Summary. One must conclude that there were no significant correlations between ability as measured by the psychological test and attitude as determined by the Remmers-Kelley scale for which the good attitude was the average of informed experts' scores. Furthermore, there was no significant difference between the correlations between ability and good attitude for the experimental students after discussion and the control students after restudy.

DOUBTS CONCERNING THE EFFICACY OF THE REMMERS-KELLEY ATTITUDE SCALE

The exposition of results obtained from the use of the attitude scale has shown that the experimental procedure produced a significant change in attitude score at one important step only, after reading the information pamphlet. Is it possible that the scale was lacking in sensitivity at the positive end? That is, were small changes in a positive attitude not detected by the scale? On the other hand, may it be that for the experimental population and for the experimental task the reading of the materials produced all the change in attitude that one could expect? It may be that general attitude toward the best parole system was not subject to significant additional change following the initial study of the materials. We have seen, however, that the ranking score was subject to additional change. And in most cases it is probably right to infer that a change in ranking the solution was accompanied by a change in specific attitude (if not in general attitude as measured by the Remmers-Kelley scale). One might well expect this change in specific attitude, if present, to be reflected in changes in the generalized scale. We have seen, however, that no such significant changes occurred. Now, it may be that the scale was sufficiently discriminating to detect the first large change in attitude due to experience with the information pamphlet, yet not discriminating enough to detect changes around the point reached after reading. What does an examination of the scale itself reveal? The mean initial attitude score was —1.14 for the experimental students and —1.22 for the control students. These points lie between statements twenty and twenty-one on the scale of forty-five statements. The lower (negative) half of the scale, then, was of little use in the experiment. Neither were the most positive items. No student's score after reading was represented by any of the five most positive items, and only twenty-four of 265 experimental students and nine of sixty-nine controls had scores represented by the twenty-five most negative items. Consequently, after the reading of the second day practically all students being already fairly positive and not likely to accept the extremely positive statements were in the position of being confined in their choices to fifteen statements. The most positive of these statements had a score value of 1.2 (10.5 on the Remmers-Kelley scoring key). The most negative had a score value of —1.1 (8.2 on the Remmers-Kelley scoring key). As scored, then, there was a range of only 2.3 points within which the students might have been expected to change. After reading alone 241 of the 265 experimental students and sixty of the sixty-nine control students came within this range. It is not surprising, then, that no additional significant changes were recorded.

Even when these considerations are given due weight there is the possibility that for the particular population considering the particular problem no additional change might have been expected. In order to see whether additional changes might have been present which the scale was not detecting, the second method of studying attitude described in Chapter II was substituted in Experiment B for the Remmers-Kelley scale. The attitude findings secured by this method in Experiment B are presented in the following pages.

II. EXPERIMENT B

In Experiment B the measure of attitude consisted of rated free expressions of attitude toward the best parole system. The nature of these free expressions, the method by which they were secured, and the method of rating them have been discussed in Chapter II. Here it is sufficient to indicate that the average rating of the experts' free expressions was considered the good attitude and was given a value of zero in scoring. Students' attitude scores, then, were all stated with reference to the experts' standard. Inasmuch as free expressions of attitude toward the best parole system known were secured at every stage at which the Remmers-Kelley scale was used in Experiment A, the rated free expressions make it possible to compare the results of the two experiments. A score of zero represents a definitely positive attitude but not extremely so. A score of —14 represents a neutral opinion. Scores greater than —14 represent negative opinions. Positive opinions range from approximately —13 or —12 to plus 7.

GAINS IN ATTITUDE SCORE

Table XIII summarizes the essential data with reference to the attitude scores at each measurement of the students in Experiment B. The scores for the first day are initial scores before the start of the experiment. Those for the second day were taken after both experimental and control students had spent a class period reading the information pamphlet. For the experimental students the third day's scores were secured after discussion in groups of four students. The control students' scores for the third day were taken after restudy of the information pamphlet. The fourth day's scores were secured after an interval of one month. The number of students is the same throughout Table XIII, 194 experimental students and 144 control students.

Just as in Experiment A at the start of the experiment, before the presentation of any experimental materials or procedures, both the experimental and the control students had mean attitudes significantly more negative than the experts. The mean in each case was much larger than three times its standard error. The difference between the experimental and the control subjects (1.51, the controls being initially closer to the experts' attitude) was probably due to chance or to some unmeasured background factors. This difference had a standard error of 0.87 and a critical ratio of 1.74. While not a reliable difference, it was somewhat larger than one would expect to find very often.

After reading (second day's score) the means of both the experimental and the control students approached more closely the experts' norm. The difference between the two groups was negligible at this point. The difference of 0.14 had a standard error of 0.69 and a critical ratio of 0.20. Interpreted, this means that there was at this stage of the experiment no significant difference between the controls and the experimentals. The discrepancy noted on the initial scores had apparently disappeared. And inasmuch as the experimental procedures to this point were identical, the groups were expected to be equal.

After discussion the mean of the experimental students approached still more closely the experts' norm; the control students' mean was also coming closer after the restudy of the information materials. Although the experimental (discussing) students at the

TABLE XIII

*Summary of Means, Sigmas, and Standard Errors of Means
for Each Day's Attitude Scores, Experiment B*

Stage of Experiment	EXPERIMENTAL SS			CONTROL SS		
	M	σ	σ_M	M	σ	σ_M
1st day	−7.43	7.62	0.55	−5.92	8.06	0.68
2nd day	−4.81	6.31	0.45	−4.95	6.24	0.52
3rd day	−3.22	6.13	0.44	−3.91	6.91	0.58
4th day	−3.76	6.43	0.47	−4.61	7.18	0.01

TABLE XIV

*Summary of Means, Sigmas, and Standard Errors of Means for
Changes in Attitude Scores at Each Stage of Experiment B*

Stage of Experiment	EXPERIMENTAL SS			CONTROL SS		
	M	σ	σ_M	M	σ	σ_M
Days 1-2 (after reading)	2.98	6.96	0.50	2.00	6.89	0.58
Days 2-3 (after discussion or restudy)	0.63	4.56	0.33	0.03	4.71	0.39
Days 3-4 (after one-month interval)	−0.45	4.79	0.35	−0.24	4.86	0.41

end of the third day had a mean score 0.69 points closer to the experts' standard, the difference was unreliable, having a standard error of 0.73 and a critical ratio of only 0.95. On the basis of the mean attitude scores, then, we must conclude that the discussing students did not gain significantly more in attitude score than the restudying students.

After the month's interval both groups had a loss in mean score with reference to the good attitude. The difference in mean scores at this point was 0.85 in favor of the experimental discussing students. This difference had a standard error of 0.77 and a critical ratio of 1.14. Interpreted, this difference was unreliable, there being thirteen chances in 100 that the true difference was zero or in favor of the control students.

In Table XIV these same data are treated somewhat differently. Whereas in Table XIII the data pertain to the attitude scores, here the data are with reference to *changes* in attitude from one measurement to the next. They are, of course, changes with reference to the experts' standard. In Table XIII the *scores* were tabulated with regard to the direction of deviation from the norm. In Table XIV *changes* in scores were tabulated with regard to the extent of the deviation from the norm but without regard to the direction of that deviation. This accounts for what appear to be discrepancies in the two tables. Examination of Table XIV reveals again the fairly large gain made after reading by both the experimental and the control students, the slight gain made by the experimentals after discussion, and the slight loss incurred by both the groups after the one-month interval. The change for the control students after restudy was a slight gain.

Were these changes in attitude as represented by the rated free expressions of attitude reliable? Only two mean changes were as much as three times as large as their standard errors. These were the changes for the experimental and control subjects after reading. The gains in which we are mainly interested, those after discussion and those after restudy, were unreliable. The discussing students made a gain of 0.63 with a standard error of the mean of 0.33 and a critical ratio of 1.91. The control students had a mean gain after restudy of 0.03. The standard error of the mean was 0.39, the critical ratio only 0.08. Since the usual standard for reliability requires a critical ratio of approximately three, we must conclude that these changes following discussion and restudy were unreliable. After the interval of one month the experimental students had an unreliable loss in good attitude. The critical ratio between the mean change of —0.45 and its standard error of 0.35 was 1.29. For the same period the controls also had an unreliable loss; the critical ratio between the mean change of —0.24 and its standard error of 0.41 was only 0.57.

About the only conclusion which can be drawn from the data of Table XIV is that there was a definitely reliable gain after reading the information pamphlet the second day. On subsequent days there were slight changes which might have been due to chance.

In view of the fact that the mean changes in attitude except that following reading were unreliable, we may infer that the differences between the changes made by the students who discussed and those who restudied were also unreliable. There are two differences in which we are interested, that at the conclusion of the third day after the experimentals discussed and after the controls restudied and that after the one-month interval. Table XIV shows that after the experimentals discussed they had a mean gain of 0.63. After the controls restudied they had a gain of 0.03. The difference was 0.60 in favor of the discussing students. This difference had a standard error of 0.51 and a critical ratio of 1.18. Consequently, for all practical purposes as shown by the computations of the scores secured by rated free expressions of attitude there was no reliable difference which can with assurance be attributed to the fact that the experimental students discussed.

The difference between the changes in attitude score relative to the experts' standard after the one-month interval was 0.21, the controls losing less than the experimentals during the interval. This difference had a standard error of 0.54 and a critical ratio of only 0.39. Again the difference between the control and the experimental students was unreliable.

Summary. We must then conclude that on the basis of the rated free expressions of attitude there were no significant differences in changes made by those who read and discussed and those who read and restudied. With the problem considered and with the population included the measure showed significant changes after reading and at no other time.

GAINS IN ATTITUDE SCORES FOR TWO ABILITY GROUPS

Did the rated free expressions of attitude show reliable differences between the two ability groups? These two ability groups, as previously explained, were the low-ability group with Ohio State University Psychological Test, Form 20 scores ranging from 10 to 39 and the high-ability group with similar test scores ranging from 70 to 150. Tables XV, XVI, and XVII summarize the data on gains in attitude score (1) after reading, (2) after discussing or restudying, and (3) after the interval of one month. By comparing the size of the standard error of each mean with the mean, one can readily see which groups made significant gains at the various stages of the experiment.

The experimental students of low ability (Table XV) had a fairly reliable gain from reading. The critical ratio was 2.47. The experimental students of high ability made a definitely reliable gain from reading, the critical ratio of the mean gain of 3.37 and the standard error of 0.81 being 4.16. The low-ability control group had an unreliable gain from reading, the critical ratio being only slightly more than one. It will be recalled that the control group had for some reason more appropriate attitudes on the first measurement than did the experimental students. This lack of reliable gain from reading probably represented a smoothing out process which made the groups equal after reading. The high-ability control group had a fairly reliable gain from reading, the critical ratio between the mean of 2.93 and the standard error of 1.03 being 2.84.

A comparison of the standard error of each mean with its mean change (Table XVI) shows that neither the high- nor the low-ability groups, experimental or control, made reliable gains after discussion or restudy. The largest critical ratio, 2.02, was for the high-ability experimental students from discussing.

A similar examination of Table XVII leads to the same conclusion. Neither low- nor high-ability groups made significant changes after the interval of one month. The greatest change was the mean loss of the high-ability experimental group, —0.78. The standard error, however, was 0.53 and the critical ratio only 1.47. Consequently, even this largest change was unreliable.

We must, then, conclude, that there were no significant attitude changes after discussion, restudy, or the one-month interval as measured by the rated free expressions of attitude for either low- or high-ability control and experimental students. For the problem considered and for the population included there were

TABLE XV

Summary of Data on Gains in Attitude Score from Reading
for Two Ability Groups of the Experimental and
Control Subjects, Experiment B Only

Ability Group	N	M	σ	σ_M
Low experimental............	50	2.64	7.53	1.07
High experimental...........	73	3.37	6.93	0.81
Low control.................	37	−0.81	4.50	0.74
High control................	45	2.93	6.89	1.03

TABLE XVI

Summary of Data on Gains in Attitude Score for Two Ability Groups,
the Experimental Subjects from Discussing and the Control
Subjects from Restudying, Experiment B Only

Ability Group	N	M	σ	σ_M
Low experimental............	49	0	5.39	0.77
High experimental...........	73	0.99	4.22	0.49
Low control.................	37	0.81	5.34	0.88
High control................	45	−0.60	3.27	0.49

TABLE XVII

Summary of Data on Gains in Attitude Score for Two Ability
Groups of the Experimental and Control Subjects After
One-Month Interval, Experiment B Only

Ability Group	N	M	σ	σ_M
Low experimental............	49	0.24	5.01	0.72
High experimental...........	69	−0.78	4.38	0.53
Low control.................	36	0	1.86	0.31
High control................	45	−0.13	3.41	0.51

reliable or near-reliable changes following the reading of the information pamphlet and at no other stage of the experiment.

Since we have found no reliable changes for low- and high-ability groups after discussion or restudy and after the month's interval, we can hardly expect to find reliable differences between groups. The differences in mean attitude score gain for various comparisons between the two ability groups of the experimental and control students are presented and evaluated in terms of their standard errors in Table XVIII. A glance at the column indicating critical ratios (column three) shows no critical ratio equaled or exceeded three, the usual standard of significance. Only two had a critical ratio larger than two. The difference between the low- and the high-ability controls from reading had a critical ratio of 2.94, closely approaching reliability. This almost reliable difference must be discounted on the previously mentioned grounds that the control group was superior to the experimental group on the initial measurement. And this superiority was apparent primarily in the low-ability controls, because although the high-ability controls gained in attitude after reading, the controls and the experimentals were practically equal at this stage. The other difference which had a critical ratio exceeding two was that for the high-ability experimental students after discussing as compared with the high-ability control after restudying. The difference was 1.59 favoring the high-ability experimental students.

TABLE XVIII

Differences in Mean Attitude Score Gain for Two Ability Groups of the Experimental and Control Subjects Evaluated in Terms of the Standard Errors of Those Differences

M minus M	d	σd	$d/\sigma d$
Low control from reading minus high control from reading....................................	−3.74	1.27	2.94
Low control from restudy minus high control from restudy.......................................	1.41	1.01	1.40
Low control after one-month interval minus high control after one-month interval................	0.13	0.60	0.22
Low experimental from reading minus high experimental from reading............................	−0.73	1.34	0.54
Low experimental from discussing minus high experimental from discussing.....................	−0.99	0.91	1.09
Low experimental after one-month interval minus high experimental after one-month interval......	1.02	0.89	1.15
Low experimental from discussing minus low control from restudy.................................	−0.81	1.17	0.69
High experimental from discussing minus high control from restudy.................................	1.59	0.69	2.30
Low experimental after one-month interval minus low control after one-month interval............	0.24	0.78	0.31
High experimental after one-month interval minus high control after one-month interval...........	−0.65	0.74	0.88

The standard error of the difference was 0.69 and the critical ratio 2.30. Interpreted, this means that there are about ninety-nine chances in 100 that this represented a real difference.

Summary. We must, then, conclude that the differences between the ability groups, experimental and control, were without significance. The only exception is the possibility that the high-ability experimental students after discussion were superior to the high-ability controls after restudy. There are ninety-nine chances in 100 that there was a real difference here. With the problem considered and the population included there were reliable or near-reliable changes in attitude after reading and at no subsequent stage of the experiment.

CORRELATIONS BETWEEN ABILITY SCORES AND ATTITUDE SCORES

Inasmuch as in Experiment B little difference in attitude of ability groups was found between those who discussed and those who restudied, it is unlikely that there were any very high correlations between ability and goodness of attitude score. The computations have, nevertheless, been made, and are here presented. The ability scores are the raw scores of the Ohio State University Psychological Test, Form 20. The attitude scores are the rated free expressions of attitude scored as deviations from the experts' standard of zero. In the correlation computations the absolute values of the deviations were considered without regard to sign. The Pearson product-moment method was used in every instance.

The correlation between ability and goodness of attitude score for all students at the beginning of the experiment before either reading or discussing occurred was — .08 ± .04. After reading the correlation for all students was — .03 ± .04. After discussion the experimental subjects had a correlation between ability and goodness of attitude score of .07 ± .05. After restudy the control students had a correlation of — .04 ± .06. Only in the case of the correlation between ability and goodness of attitude score at the beginning of the experiment—before either reading or discussion had occurred—was the *r* as much as twice the size of the probable error. And since for reliability the correlation should be at least four times the probable error, no one of the correlations was reliable. The r's might have been larger after reading, discussion, and restudy had not a large number of students had attitude scores closely approximating the experts' norm.

When one considers the difference in correlation for those who discussed and those who restudied, one finds similar results. The obtained difference between the r's after discussion and restudy was 0.11, the experimental discussing students showing a more positive correlation. The PE diff. was 0.78. The d/PE$_d$ was 0.14. Interpreted, this means that there was no reliable difference between the two groups insofar as correlation between ability and attitude was concerned.

Summary. We must then conclude that there were no significant correlations between ability as measured by the Ohio State University Psychological Test, Form 20, and the goodness of attitude as determined by the rated free expressions of attitude, the good attitude for which was the average rating of the informed experts' free expressions. Furthermore, there was no significant difference between the correlations of ability and attitude for experimental students after discussion and control students after restudy.

COMPARATIVE RESULTS OF THE TWO MEASURES OF ATTITUDE

In Chapter II it was indicated that a second measure of attitude was substituted in Experiment B for the Remmers-Kelley generalized scale because of certain doubts concerning its goodness that had arisen from its use in Experiment A. The nature of these doubts has been considered earlier in this chapter in the exposition of the findings on attitude in Experiment A. The data on attitudes for Experiment B in which the rated free expressions of attitude were the measure, make possible a comparison of results attained by the two methods and an evaluation of the doubts raised.

The comparative findings with respect to mean attitude scores will first be considered. In both experiments both the control students and the experimental students had initial attitudes significantly less positive than the experts' attitude. After reading the scores of both the experimental and the control subjects approached more closely the experts' norm. After discussion the experimental students in Experiment B approached still more closely the good attitude; those of Experiment A fell away slightly. After restudy the control students in Experiment A and Experiment B made a slight additional approach toward the experts' standard. After the one-month interval the experimental students of Experiments A and B had mean attitude scores that had moved slightly away from the experts' norm. The control students of Experiment A and those of Experiment B lost slightly during this period. With respect to mean attitude scores at the various stages of the experiments we must conclude that the two measures of attitude gave approximately the same results. The differences were negligible.

We find similar results when the findings of Experiments A and B with respect to mean *changes* in attitude from one stage of the experiment to another are compared. For both experiments the gains made after reading the information pamphlet were reliable. No other changes were reliable. Slight changes after discussion, after restudy, and after the one-month interval were made in both experiments. None of these additional changes, however, was reliable. So, again, this time with respect to mean changes in attitude score from one stage of the experiment to the next, we must conclude that the two measures of attitude gave approximately the same results. So far our comparison has found the two measures of attitude agreeing in showing reliable gains in attitude after reading; at no subsequent stage of the experiment were reliable changes found.

Did the two measures of attitude agree when the reliability of the differences between mean changes was considered? In both experiments we found a difference between the students who discussed and those who restudied. In Experiment A the difference favored the students who had restudied, in Experiment B the students who had discussed. In both instances the differences were unreliable. After the one-month interval the control students who had restudied lost less than the experimental students who had discussed. In Experiment A the critical ratio for the difference was 1.79, in Experiment B 0.39, both unreliable. Once again we must conclude, this time with respect to the reliability of differences in mean changes, that the two measures of attitude gave essentially the same results. No significant differences were found by either measure.

Did the two measures of attitude give similar results with respect to gains in attitude for the two ability groups? In neither experiment were reliable gains made after discussion or after restudy. In neither experiment did we find reliable differences between ability groups of the experimental and control students. In both experiments one difference only closely approached reliability. That difference, in Experiment B, was between the mean gain for the high-ability experimental students after discussion as compared with that for the high-ability control students after restudy. Here the difference in favor of the high-ability discussing students had a critical ratio of 2.30, not high enough to be considered defintely reliable but high enough to indicate that there are about ninety-nine chances in 100 that it is a true difference. In Experiment A the corresponding difference had a critical ratio of 0.89, indicating only eighty-one chances in 100 of a true difference. With reference to differences in attitude gain for the two ability groups, we must then conclude that the two measures of attitude gave essentially the same results. No significant differences were found by either.

Did the two measures of attitude give similar correlations between attitude score and ability score? Both measures, one in each of the two experiments, showed extremely low positive or negative correlations between attitude and ability at each stage of the experiments. In both experiments the difference in correlation between ability and attitude for the experimental students after discussion and for the control students after restudy was unreliable.

FINAL COMMENTS ABOUT THE TWO MEASURES OF ATTITUDE

A comparison of the two measures of attitude, one used in Experiment A and the other in Experiment B, shows the following to be true:

1. With respect to mean attitude score at the various stages of the experiments the two measures gave approximately the same results.

2. The two measures produced approximately the same results when mean changes in attitude from one stage of the experiments to the next were considered.

3. When differences in mean changes between the students who discussed and those who restudied were considered, again the two measures gave essentially the same results. This was true of the differences at the end of the third day as well as one month later.

4. No significant differences in attitude gain for the two ability groups were found in either experiment by either attitude measure.

5. Both measures in both experiments showed significant gains in attitude after reading the information pamphlet and at no other stage of the experiment.

What is the logical conclusion about the doubts raised in regard to the Remmers-Kelley scale after using it in Experiment A? The following doubts were raised: Was it lacking in sensitivity at the positive end of the scale? Why should the ranking score and not the attitude score change significantly as a result of discussion?

These questions cannot be answered definitely. A few comments at this time about each one are, however, appropriate. Was the Remmers-Kelley scale lacking in sensitivity at the positive end of the scale? It was noted that the scale seemed limited at the positive end. The free expression of attitude technique seemed to remedy this, for, as rated, the free expressions of attitude had scores ranging from three to thirty. Neutral opinions were given a rating of nine, leaving twenty-one degrees of positive statement, all of which represented the attitudes of a large number of students. Obviously here there was plenty of room for change, a matter which was very doubtful with reference to the Remmers-Kelley scale. Even though it appears that the rated free expressions of attitude were more sensitive, nevertheless this factor apparently did not enter into the results, for both measures produced esentially the same results. The two measures were apparently equally good.

Why should the ranking score change significantly as a result of discussion without a corresponding change in attitude? It may be, of course, that both measures of attitude were equally faulty. On the contrary, for the particular population, social problem, and experimental procedures it may be that all the change in attitude which might be expected was registered after reading. It must be remembered that both measures dealt with general attitudes. General attitudes may change rapidly on the basis of relatively slight experiences and may be subject to relatively little additional change in the same direction on the basis of additional experiences. Specific attitudes, however, are presumably subject to additional change, granting that the assumption is true, namely, that the ranking of solutions constituted in part a measure of changes in specific attitudes toward particular systems of releasing convicts.

Assuming that the two measures of attitude were valid and that no changes in general attitude were present, we are faced with an important question with reference to the relationship between attitude and action. The measure of choice of solution was very similar to an action situation. We have noted reliable changes after discussion with this measure. We have detected no changes after discussion with the measures of attitude. It appears, then, that the relationship between attitude as measured and action as measured is far from a one to one relationship. When attitudes are considered as having a one to one relationship with action, the assumption is that the action choices are universal. It is probable, however, that most action situations do not permit universal choices, that such situations involve a limited number of possible choices only. If this difference between attitude and action is a true one, a one to one relationship in most instances cannot be expected. Consequently, attitude measures should be used as indicative of probable action only when due discretion is exercised.

Finally, another possible reason for the lack of significant change except after reading presents itself. The lack may have been due to the vagueness of the attitude stimulus, "the best parole system known." Instead of changes in attitude changes in the definition of the best parole system may have occurred.

Summary. The failure to find significant changes in general attitude except after reading may have been due then to (1) faulty measures, (2) lack of such changes being present, or (3) a vagueness in the attitude stimulus.

CHAPTER V

ADDITIONAL FINDINGS

IN THIS chapter are presented certain findings which had no place in the previous chapters. These additional findings are of two types: (a) those pertaining to relationships between ranking scores and attitude scores at the various stages of the experiment, and (b) those having to do with the effect of information and discussion on proficiency in evaluating the characteristics of solutions to the social problem.

CORRELATIONS BETWEEN RANKING SCORES AND ATTITUDE SCORES

We have noted in the two preceding chapters very low but significant correlations between general ability and good ranking scores and very low insignificant correlations between general ability and good attitude scores. It is pertinent to inquire whether there was any relationship between goodness of ranking score and goodness of attitude score. The r's for Experiment A and Experiment B for this relationship at each stage of the experiment are given below:

Stage of Experiment and Subjects	r for	
	Experiment A	Experiment B
1st day, all subjects	.03 ± .04	—.04 ± .04
2nd day, all subjects	.33 ± .03	.32 ± .03
3rd day, experimental subjects	.35 ± .04	.34 ± .04
3rd day, control subjects	.42 ± .07	.38 ± .05
4th day, experimental subjects	.29 ± .04	.15 ± .05
4th day, control subjects	.37 ± .07	.41 ± .05

It will be noted that there was practically no relationship on the first day at the time of the initial measurements. Since for re-

liability the r should be at least four times its probable error, these
initial correlations were unreliable. On succeeding days the r's
were, with one exception, more than four times the size of their
probable errors. The one exception is that for the Experiment B
experimental subjects on the fourth day, one month after the
completion of the experiment. The r's show a tendency for good
attitude scores to be associated with good ranking scores after
reading, after discussion or restudy, and after a one-month interval, but not on the initial measurement. Considering each experiment separately, one notes that there were reliable changes in the
r's from the first to the second day, that is, from the initial measurements to those made after reading the information pamphlet.
In Experiment A this change in relationship was such that the
value of d/PE_d was 6.00. The corresponding d/PE_d for Experiment B was 5.60. Both were well over four, the usual standard of
significance. No other changes were statistically significant. The
differences in the r's of the experimental students and the control
students on the third day and on the fourth day were not significant in either experiment. The largest difference, 0.26 between the
Experiment B controls and experimentals on the fourth day had
a d/PE_d of 3.71, somewhat short of the standard for significance.

Summary. After reading the information pamphlet the subjects
of both experiments had r's indicating some tendency for good
ranking scores to accompany good attitude scores. After discussion or restudy and after the one-month interval no significant
changes in the relationship occurred. The experimental subjects
did not differ significantly from the control subjects.

PROFICIENCY IN EVALUATING THE CHARACTERISTICS
OF SOLUTIONS

In this section we come to a consideration of the final question
listed in Chapter I: Were the subjects who studied and discussed
as proficient in evaluating the characteristics of solutions to the
parole problem as those who read and restudied? The nature of
the test used, the method of constructing it, and the method of
scoring it were discussed in Chapter II. Here it is sufficient to indicate that it was administered at the end of the third day in Ex-

periment B only. The 194 experimental students took it after discussing in small groups. The 144 control students took it after restudying the information pamphlet. Until the third day of the experiment the procedure for both experimental and control students was identical. Did the students who studied and discussed do better on the test than those who studied and restudied? With a possible score of 30 the experimental students had a mean score of 20.39. The standard deviation of the distribution was 5.03, the standard error of the mean 0.36. The mean score for the control students was 20.12. The standard deviation of this distribution was 4.33, the standard error of the mean 0.36. The mean scores for both groups were far better than one would expect from chance. Both groups were apparently fairly well able to evaluate the characteristics of a good method of releasing convicts from prison according to the standard set by the experts. The difference between the means was slight, being 0.27 in favor of the experimental students. The standard error of the difference was 0.51. The resulting critical ratio was only 0.53. The difference was consequently very unreliable.

Summary. On the basis of this test there was no significant difference in the ability of the two groups in evaluating the characteristics of solutions to the parole problem. For the particular problem, population, and procedures those who discussed did not do significantly better than those who restudied.

CHAPTER VI

SUMMARY AND IMPLICATIONS

CHAPTER I indicated that this study was an attempt to evaluate in part the assumption that discussion in addition to information is essential for the wise decision on and the appropriate attitude toward a controversial social problem. There it was indicated that this research had to do with some of the outcomes of discussion, outcomes in terms of the individual's attitudes and choices. In this final chapter the findings of the study will be summarized and assayed in terms of the purpose of the research.

SUMMARY OF PROCEDURE

The Problem. The problem of the research has been implied in the statements above. More specifically, the study attempted to determine experimentally whether information on and discussion of a social problem cumulatively contribute to appropriate attitudes and appropriate solutions. Answers were sought to specific questions pertaining to the effect of information and discussion on choice of solution to a social problem, to the effect of information and discussion on attitude toward a social problem, and to the effect of information and discussion on proficiency in evaluating the characteristics of the solutions to a social problem.

The Subjects. The subjects of the two experiments were 672 high school juniors and seniors enrolled in courses in American history, social problems, and sociology. Of these, 334 were in Experiment A, 338 in Experiment B. Of the students in Experiment A, 265 were used as experimental subjects, 69 as controls. In Experiment B 194 students were in the experimental group, 144 in the control group.

The Experimental Materials. Experimental materials for the experiments included the problem for study and discussion, tools of measurement, and a body of factual information. The problem selected for discussion was one for which the *good* answer was determinable by a consensus of expert judgment. As finally worded it was: "What, if anything, should be done about Ohio's system of releasing convicts from prison?" It is obviously a controversial social problem. To make sure that it would be interesting to the subjects of the experiment and within their range of comprehension, a trial was made with similar subjects.

Two measures of attitude were used: (1) the Remmers-Kelley generalized "Scale for Measuring Attitude toward Any Institution" and (2) free expressions of attitude toward the best parole system. The first was used in Experiment A, the other in Experiment B. With both measures the good or appropriate attitude was the average of informed experts' scores.

The measure of choice of solution contained five alternative solutions to the problem. All five were ranked by the students. The good ranking was the ranking made by informed experts.

A test for evaluating the characteristics of solutions was constructed by collecting characteristics and submitting them to experts. No characteristic was included in the final form of the test if more than one of the experts disagreed on its evaluation.

A mimeographed body of factual information on the social problem was prepared. It was based on writings on the subject, interviews with informed experts, and correspondence with the experts. These experts also reviewed the pamphlet for accuracy and completeness. The body of information was purely factual, every attempt having been made to avoid the use of opinion and interpretation.

The Procedure. In procedure the two experiments, A and B, were essentially the same. After initial measurements of attitude and choice of solution all students, both experimental and control, read the body of factual information. After the reading measurements of attitude and solution were again made. On the basis of the ranking of solution score made after reading, the experimental students were divided into groups of four for discussion of the problem. The body of information was available for reference during the discussions. While the experimental students were discussing, the control group restudied the body of factual information. After the restudy or discussion the measures of attitude and solution were again administered. After a one-month interval the same measurements were again made.

Experiment B differed from Experiment A in the following respects: The class periods, and consequently the reading, discussion, and restudy periods, were somewhat shorter than in Experiment A. A free expression of attitude was substituted for the Remmers-Kelley scale. After discussion or restudy a test of ability to evaluate the characteristics of methods of releasing convicts was added to the measures administered. Other differences included a slight change in handling the restudy of the control group and in the use of undisguised measures of attitude and solution initially.

The Data Secured. By the use of the materials, measures, and procedures briefly described above the following data were gathered:

1. Initial attitude and ranking scores.
2. Attitude and ranking scores after an opportunity to read the body of information.
3. Attitude and ranking scores of the experimental students after discussion and the same scores for the control students after an opportunity to restudy the pamphlet.
4. Group ranking scores of the experimental students after discussion.
5. Scores on the test of ability to evaluate the characteristics of solutions for the experimental students after discussion and for the control students after restudy (Experiment B only).
6. Attitude and ranking scores one month after the completion of the experiment proper.

In addition, psychological test scores were available in the office files of both schools.

Limitations of the Research. The findings of the research, which will be reviewed in the following pages, must be considered with reference to the limitations of the research. The findings may properly be applied to the type of population used as experimental subjects, young adults without formal training in discussion techniques and presumably with rather superficial initial attitudes toward the problem considered. The findings are further limited to the type of problem discussed and studied and to the type of discussion used in the experiment. One must also remember that the good attitude and the good ranking of the solutions were each a consensus of expert judgment. Finally, the experimental situation was simplified by presenting factual information free from the usual interpretations and persuasive techniques. The findings might well have been different with other types of population, with different procedures, with other types of problem, with other types of discussion, and with the information mingled with interpretation in its presentation.

SUMMARY OF FINDINGS

Findings Pertaining to Choices of Solution

1. Both the students who read and discussed and those who read and restudied made reliable gains in ranking the given solutions to the parole problem. The discussing students gained reliably more after discussion than the control students after restudy.

2. All types of subjects—good, intermediate, and poor with respect to ranking score after reading—showed gains in ranking score regardless of the type of student with whom they discussed. Good students were seldom pulled down after discussing with poor students. Poor students gained even after discussing with their fellows. The gains for all types except the good, who could gain very little, were significant. Good students improved more after discussing with other good students than after discussing with intermediate or poor students. The intermediate students gained more after discussing with the good students than after discussing with other intermediates or with poor students. Poor students gained more after discussing with good students than after discussing with intermediate or with other poor students. While not all the differences were reliable, analysis of variance showed a reliable trend for greatest improvement to occur when the discussions took place with companions having the best ranking scores before discussion.

3. Both high- and low-intelligence groups, experimental and control, had reliable gains in ranking score after reading. Both high- and low-intelligence groups had reliable gains following discussion but not after restudy. With reference to differences between intelligence groups the following differences were reliable: The low-ability experimental students gained more from discussion than the high-ability experimental students. Low-ability students gained more from discussion than low-ability students from restudy. The difference between the gains of the low- and high-ability students from reading, in favor of the high-ability group, closely approached reliability. Other differences were definitely unreliable.

4. There was a low positive correlation between psychological test score and ranking score, highest after reading. There was no significant difference between the r for control students and that for experimental students at any stage of the experiment.

Findings Pertaining to Attitude

1. The two measures of attitude, one used in each of the two experiments, gave approximately the same results: Both measures showed a significant approach toward the good attitude after reading and at no subsequent stage of the experiment.

2. There was no significant difference between the attitudes of the experimental students after discussion and the control students after restudy.

3. There was no significant difference between the experimental students and the control students in retention of attitude after the one-month interval.

4. With reference to differences in attitude gain for the two intelligence groups of the experimental and control subjects, no significant differences were found in either experiment with either attitude measure.

5. Both measures of attitude showed extremely low positive or negative correlations between attitude and intelligence. In no instance was the correlation high enough in relation to the size of the probable error to be considered even slightly indicative of a relationship.

Additional Findings

1. After reading and at subsequent stages of the experiment all subjects of both experiments showed a tendency for good ranking scores to accompany good attitude scores. Except for the change from before to after reading there were no significant changes in the correlations. The differences in the correlations between the experimental and the control students were not significant.

2. After discussion or restudy both experimental and control groups showed a proficiency far beyond chance expectations in evaluating the characteristics of the solutions. Although the experimental students were slightly more proficient in evaluating the characteristics than the controls, the difference was definitely unreliable.

IMPLICATIONS AND QUALITATIVE COMMENTS

What do we now think of the assumption that discussion in addition to information is essential to the wise decision on and the appropriate attitude toward a controversial social problem? The findings just summarized indicate the best answer that can now be stated: For the particular population considering the parole problem according to the procedures used, discussion in addition to information more often resulted in an approximation of the good decision. Those who merely studied, however, improved their choices of solution significantly, although their improvement was significantly less than that of the discussing students. When attitude is considered, the findings do not support the assumption. For the particular population, problem, and procedures there were no significant differences in attitude between those who read and discussed and those who read and restudied. Consequently, the assumption appears to be only partially true. Whether the same results would occur with other types of populations, problems, procedures, and measures we do not know.

To What Influences Were the Results Due? In Chapter I it was noted that not all the factors or influences involved in a discussion situation are inherent parts of such a situation. It is pertinent to consider briefly the probable influences at work in the experimental discussions reported in this study. Active learning, the averaging process, and the prestige of majorities were mentioned as influences not exclusive to discussion and readily obtainable without discussion. Is it probable that the superiority in ranking score of the discussing subjects over the restudying subjects was due to these factors? It is unlikely that active learning was responsible, for active learning was also present in the tasks given the control subjects on the day of the restudy. Consequently, there is considerable assurance that any influence of active learning present in the discussion was also largely present in the restudy. Thus this factor cannot account for the difference in ranking score. It is also unlikely that the averaging factor accounted for all the difference, although it is possible that it was involved in a degree. The nature of the problem discussed made averaging of points of view somewhat difficult, although not impossible. Group scores, which would be most likely to reflect the averaging process, were not used in the comparisons. If the averaging factor was very influential, one would have expected the individuals with the better scores before discussion to be pulled down by the discussion with individuals with the poorer scores. Such was, however, not the case. If any leveling occurred, it was largely a leveling upward. Nevertheless, to some degree the averaging factor may have been involved. This point merits further study. Was the prestige of the majority a factor influencing the results? In this research there was no direct evidence on this point. Groups were constructed without attention to the majority factor. Inasmuch as they were composed of all good, poor, or intermediate individuals (with reference to ranking score after reading) or of two of these types in equal numbers, it is probable that the influence of majorities was slight in the experimental discussions. The factor could, however, have been present, for within the groups as composed there was the possibility of individuals of like scores differing on the particular choices in such a way that majorities were possible. Hence, although there is no direct evidence on the majority factor, its presence remains entirely possible.

If, as is probable, these factors which are not peculiar to discussion were not responsible for all of the differences in ranking score, it becomes probable that factors inherent in the discussion situation caused at least part of the differences. The larger number of interpretations and the wider range of criticism of interpretations and reasons probably caused the discussing students to have better ranking scores than the students who worked alone. All of these factors which possibly influenced the results merit much additional study.

Application of the Results. To what extent can the results of the research be applied? Within the limitations previously discussed the results certainly may be applied. The findings are perhaps not applicable to all life situations, particularly those in which the facts on the problem have been secured mingled with propaganda, persuasion, and interpretation. Further study would be necessary to determine whether the same results would accrue in such situations. It is possible that in such situations the discussers would show even greater superiority over those who do not discuss. For the criticism of the discussers might well correct the effects of incorrect interpretations and might well counter propaganda and persuasion leading to wrong solutions. The non-discussers, at least many of them, might well fall prey to incorrect interpretations and persuasive techniques which point toward incorrect solutions. It is probable, too, that the discussers would show a greater superiority if both groups had to collect their own facts. For again the information secured would be mingled with interpretation and persuasion with the likelihood of the discussers' being better able to arrive at correct interpretations and solutions. Moreover, if the students collected their own information, it is probable that not all would collect all the pertinent facts. The discussers then would profit by information possessed by other members of the group. The non-discussers would be limited to the knowledge they themselves had collected and would be unable to profit by the knowledge of their fellows.

Pending further research we can perhaps apply the results in the classroom with the greatest assurance. The area of the social studies presents the best opportunity. For in that area controversial social problems are common. Students of high school age for the most part probably do not have very deep-seated attitudes toward the problems. The facts can be made available, and on the basis of the facts the students may discuss and arrive at their own conclusions. Such a method, analogous to the procedure in this research except for the measurements, appears to be ideal for handling controversial social problems for which the good answer is known or unknown but which arouse much community criticism if the teacher tries to teach in traditional ways *his* answer to the problem.

The use of such a method in the classroom is justified not only on the basis of the objective findings of the research here reported but also on the basis of certain qualitative findings. It has already been noted that those who discuss are superior in ability to arrive at the good solution and that the discussion is particularly valuable to those of low intelligence. These were objective findings. Considering qualitative ones, the writer feels that the students prefer the discussion. In an earlier chapter it was pointed out that crestfallen expressions greeted the experimenter when he announced restudy in the control classes. Not only through facial expression but through words as well the students conveyed the very definite impression of preferring discussion to restudy. The discussion is apparently more enjoyable, combining real improvement with intellectual fellowship. Furthermore, it is extremely doubtful whether motivation to secure co-operation on the restudy procedure could be exercised over a long period of time. In the research reported the experimenter feels that he secured unusual co-operation.

Inference with Reference to Democracy. No single study should be used as a base from which to make far-reaching inferences. Consequently, the writer hesitates to make inferences from the study with reference to democracy. He does feel, however, that some of the findings at least point in the direction of upholding the democratic way of doing things. Democracy, which at least in theory gives the citizens the duty of making choices on problems common to the people, appears to assume that the average citizen is, through oral and written discussion, capable of arriving at good decisions. The findings of this research support the assumption. The students of low intelligence arrived at good solutions practically as well as those of high intelligence, a process which discussion appeared to facilitate. The correlation between intelligence and ability to rank the given solutions was very low. Furthermore, students with wrong answers improved their answers a great deal after discussion, even when that discussion was with other individuals with wrong answers. Students with good answers were seldom pulled down after discussing with students with poor answers. These findings, of course, do not prove that democracy is good; they merely lend support to the democratic way. The weakness in the argument is that in the experiments here reported the students were given the facts free from persuasion, propaganda, and interpretation, whereas in real life individuals are seldom given the facts. And when they are given the facts, those facts are often incomplete and mingled with persuasion or biased interpretations. There is a rebuttal to this counterargument; namely, that in life situations where persuasion is mingled with the facts discussion may be even more valuable. This last point was made at greater length in the last section.

Research with Controversial Problems. In Chapter II the difficulties of research with controversial problems were mentioned. Inasmuch as few researches have ventured to use such experimental tasks and inasmuch as the writer has ventured to use one, this study should not close without a brief consideration of the feasibility of using such tasks in research in the area of discussion. The writer feels that it is feasible to use controversial problems as experimental tasks. There appears to be no other way of simulating life situations. He grants that the use of them is difficult and open to some criticism. Those problems which have answers on which experts may be expected to agree appear to be few. But if the researcher goes to the trouble of finding controversial tasks on which a large proportion of the highly informed do agree, he will be able to conduct research the findings of which will have more application than if non-controversial tasks are used. If the highly informed experts in the area of the task are in close agreement, there is justification for considering their answer the good one.

Suggestions for Further Study. Both in this chapter and in Chapter II comments have been made which show the need for additional study. At this point these may well be collected as suggestions for further study. They are presented as questions:

1. Would the findings be different if all subjects had been presented facts mingled with propaganda and interpretation?
2. What would be the results if both discussers and non-discussers had collected their own information?
3. Would well-trained discussers have shown a similar or greater superiority over non-discussers?
4. What would be the effect on the findings if the subjects had deep-seated prejudices on the problem discussed and studied?
5. Would the results have been different if the small discussion groups had been led by skilled yet non-indoctrinating leaders?
6. Does discussion facilitate the acquisition of information?
7. Does discussion develop tolerance toward those holding differing points of view?
8. Are there other educative outcomes of discussion?

SUMMARY

In this final chapter the procedure of this research and the findings have been summarized. On the basis of the findings implications have been made. It was found that the students who read and discussed were better able to arrive at good solutions than those who read and restudied. No differences were found with respect to attitude and none with respect to ability to evaluate the characteristics of solutions. The results appear to be particularly applicable to classroom work in the social studies. The findings of the study may possibly lend some support to those who believe that democracy can function. The study reveals that it is feasible to use controversial lifelike social problems as experimental tasks in research in discussion. Finally, suggestions for further study which have developed from this research have been presented.

BIBLIOGRAPHY

1. BANE, C. L. "The Lecture Versus the Class Discussion Method of College Teaching." *School and Society,* Vol. 21, pp. 300-302, 1925.
2. BARTON, W. A., JR. "The Effect of Group Activity and Individual Effort in Developing Ability to Solve Problems in First-Year Algebra." *Educational Administration and Supervision,* Vol. 12, pp. 512-518, 1926.
3. BECHTEREV, W. AND LANGE, A. "Die Ergebnisse des Experiments auf dem Gebeite der kollektiven Reflexologie." *Zsch. F. angew. Psychol.,* Vol. 24, pp. 224-254, 1924.
4. BURT, H. E. "Sex Differences in the Effect of Discussion." *Journal of Experimental Psychology,* Vol. 3, pp. 390-395, 1920.
5. DASHIELL, J. F. "Experimental Studies of the Influence of Social Situations on the Behavior of Individual Human Adults." In *Handbook of Social Psychology* (C. Murchison, Ed.). Clark University Press, Worcester, 1935.
6. ELLIOTT, HARRISON S. *The Process of Group Thinking.* Association Press, New York, 1928.
7. FANSLER, THOMAS. *Discussion Methods for Adult Groups.* American Association for Adult Education, New York, 1934.
8. FOLLETT, M. P. *Creative Experience.* Longmans, Green and Co., New York, 1924.
9. FOLLETT, M. P. *The New State.* Longmans, Green and Co., New York, 1926.
10. GORDON, K. "Group Judgments in the Field of Lifted Weights." *Journal of Experimental Psychology,* Vol. 7, pp. 398-400, 1924.
11. GURNEE, H. "Maze Learning in the Collective Situation." *Journal of Experimental Psychology,* Vol. 21, pp. 106-112, 1937.
12. JENNESS, ARTHUR. "The Role of Discussion in Changing Opinion Regarding a Matter of Fact." *Journal of Abnormal and Social Psychology,* Vol. 27, pp. 279 ff., 1932.
13. JUDSON, LYMAN AND JUDSON, ELLEN. *Modern Group Discussion.* H. W. Wilson Company, New York, 1937.
14. KNIGHT, H. C. *A Comparison of the Reliability of Group and Individual Judgments.* Master's essay in Columbia University Library, 1921.
15. LEIGH, R. D. *Group Leadership.* W. W. Norton & Company, Inc., New York, 1936.

16. LINDEMAN, E. C. *Social Discovery.* Republic Publishing Co., New York, 1924.

17. LINDEMAN, E. C. *Social Education.* New Republic, Inc., New York, 1933.

18. LORGE, I. "Prestige, Attitude, and Suggestion." *Journal of Social Psychology,* Vol. 7, p. 386 ff., 1936.

19. MOORE, H. T. "The Comparative Influence of Majority and Expert Opinion." *American Journal of Psychology,* Vol. 32, pp. 16-20, 1921.

20. MURPHY, GARDNER; MURPHY, LOIS BARCLAY; AND NEWCOMB, THEODORE M. *Experimental Social Psychology.* Harper and Brothers, New York, 1937.

21. REMMERS, H. AND OTHERS. "Studies in Attitudes—A Contribution to Social Psychological Research Methods." *Studies in Higher Education XXVI, Bulletin of Purdue University,* Vol. 35, No. 4, 1934.

22. SHAW, M. E. "Comparison of Individuals and Small Groups in the Rational Solution of Complex Problems." *American Journal of Psychology,* Vol. 44, pp. 491-504, 1932.

23. SHEFFIELD, ALFRED D. *Creative Discussion.* The Inquiry, New York, 1927.

24. SHEFFIELD, ALFRED D. *Training for Group Experience.* The Inquiry, New York, 1929.

25. SIMPSON, RAY H. *A Study of Those Who Influence and of Those Who Are Influenced in Discussion.* Contributions to Education, No. 748. Bureau of Publications, Teachers College, Columbia University, New York, 1938.

26. SNEDECOR, GEORGE W. *Statistical Methods.* Collegiate Press, Ames, Iowa, 1937.

27. SOROKIN, P. A. AND BOLDYREFF, J. W. "An Experimental Study of the Influence of Suggestion on the Discrimination and the Valuation of People." *American Journal of Sociology,* Vol. 37, pp. 720-737, 1932.

28. SOUTH, M. E. "Some Psychological Aspects of Committee Work." *Journal of Applied Psychology,* Vol. 11, pp. 348-368; 437-464, 1927.

29. SPENCE, R. B. "Lecture and Class Discussion in Teaching Educational Psychology." *Journal of Educational Psychology,* Vol. 19, pp. 454-462, 1928.

30. STUDEBAKER, JOHN W. *Plain Talk.* The National Home Library Foundation, Washington, D. C., 1936.

31. THORNDIKE, R. L. "On What Type of Task Will a Group Do Well?" *Journal of Abnormal and Social Psychology,* Vol. 33, pp. 409-413, 1938.

32. THORNDIKE, R. L. "The Effect of Discussion upon the Correctness of Group Decisions, When the Factor of Majority Influence Is Allowed For." *Journal of Social Psychology*, Vol. 9, pp. 343-362, 1938.

33. WATSON, GOODWIN B. "A Comparison of Group and Individual Performance at Certain Intellectual Tasks." In *Ninth International Congress of Psychology, Proceedings and Papers, 1929*, p. 473, 1930. (Details of this research are found in item 20, pp. 730 ff.)

34. WATSON, GOODWIN B. "Do Groups Think More Effectively than Individuals?" *Journal of Abnormal and Social Psychology*, Vol. 23, pp. 328-336, 1928.

35. WIESE, MILDRED J. (in collaboration with Bryson, Lyman and Hallenbeck, Wilbur C.). *Let's Talk It Over*. University of Chicago Press, Chicago, 1936.

APPENDIX

THE PAMPHLET OF FACTUAL INFORMATION USED IN THE EXPERIMENTS

What, If Anything, Should Be Done about Ohio's System of Releasing Convicts from Prison?

BY

WILLIAM M. TIMMONS

INSTRUCTIONS TO STUDENTS

On the accompanying pages you will find (1) a page of explanation of terms used in this pamphlet and (2) some *facts* about methods of releasing convicts from prison. Detailed factual explanations of the systems used in Mississippi, New Jersey, New York, and Ohio are presented. *Read these pages carefully.* Late in the class period, on the basis of these facts you will be asked, just as you were yesterday, to rank the solutions to the problem: What, if anything, should be done about Ohio's method of releasing convicts from prison? If you have time, read the pamphlet several times. If you have any question, raise your hand; the instructor or experimenter will come to you and answer your question.

EXPLANATION OF TERMS

Parole is an activity through which prisoners who have served a portion of their sentences (prison terms) are released from prison under supervision, one condition being that they may be returned to the prison if their conduct is not acceptable. Parole is not a form of *clemency*. Acts of clemency sometimes confused with parole are pardon and commutation. *Pardon* is an act which has the effect of making the prisoner a free person. Through *commutation* the severity of the punishment for a crime is lessened.

The *parole board* is the body which under appropriate laws decides whether or not a prisoner shall be released on parole. If a man on parole (a *parolee*) violates his parole, the board may return him to prison for the length of his maximum sentence. A parolee *violates his parole* by committing a new crime or by breaking any rule made by the parole authorities. The *parole officers* are the officials who supervise the parolees.

When a prisoner's or a parolee's *sentence is terminated* or when a person is *discharged from parole,* he is free to re-enter society without supervision.

When a convicted person is given an *indeterminate prison sentence,* the amount of time to be spent in prison is not definitely set. The judge usually sets a *minimum* period and a *maximum* period; for example, a prisoner may be "sent up" (sentenced) for from five to ten years. In this case the minimum sentence is five years, the maximum sentence ten years. The indeterminate sentence system assumes that prisoners vary in their ability to be reformed and to "go straight." It also assumes that the step from prisoner to free man should be taken gradually and under supervision. Parole is normally a part of this system. The prisoner is usually *eligible for parole* after serving the minimum sentence. If paroled, he may be supervised until the end of the period set as a maximum sentence.

When a convicted person is given a *determinate (definite) prison sentence,* the time he is to serve in prison is definitely stated. Normally, he is neither eligible for parole nor supervised when released. He serves the full amount of the sentence unless he is pardoned or his sentence commuted. This system assumes that on the expiration of his sentence the prisoner is either reformed or has been sufficiently frightened by his punishment that he will "go straight" when released.

Of the several types of professional people having something to do with prisoners and with their release two perhaps need brief explanation. A *psychologist* is one who studies the behavior of individuals (including criminals); through various tests he is often able to diagnose mental and emotional strengths and weaknesses. A *psychiatrist* is a medical doctor who is versed in psychology.

EXPOSITION OF FOUR SYSTEMS OF RELEASING PRISONERS

I. *Status*

For each of the four states we are considering, the type of sentence given, the number of convicts in prison, and the number on parole are indicated below:

State	Type of Sentence Given Criminals	Number in Prison	Number on Parole
Mississippi	Definite sentences for all offenses	2,600	None
New Jersey	Indeterminate sentences mainly	3,280	4,500
New York	Indeterminate sentences mainly	14,488	8,000
Ohio	Indeterminate sentences mainly	9,392	6,000

II. *General Organization of the Prison and Parole Setups*

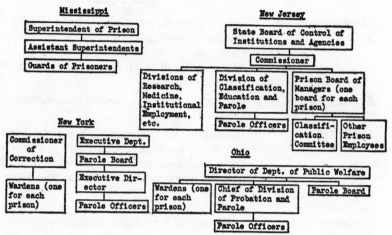

III. *Powers and Duties of the Officials*

State and Official	The Most Important Powers and Duties of the Official
Mississippi	
Prison Head Assistants	Responsible for care of prison and prisoners. Assist the prison head (the superintendent of prison).
Prison Guards	Guard prisoners, preserve order, prevent escapes, administer discipline, etc.
New Jersey	
State Board of Control (9 members)	Plans all prison and parole policies and procedures; has power to order any procedure and to transfer prisoners to other prisons or from prison to hospital as it feels will be beneficial.
Commissioner	Executes and administers policies and procedures of the State Board; assists in formulating Board's policies and procedures.
Prison Board of Managers (5-7 members)	Determines a prisoner's eligibility for parole (save where law provides for second offenders); grants and revokes parole according to State Board's policies and procedures; through prison head controls, manages, and directs the prison according to the policies of the State Board of Control.

State and Official	*The Most Important Powers and Duties of the Official*
Classification Committee	Studies convicts; sets a program of educational and work training suitable for them; recommends parole and conditions governing it; notifies parole office of new prisoners and of possible parolees.
Prison Head	Carries out programs planned by classification committee.
Parole Officers	Investigate and report new prisoners' home and social conditions; investigate and report home conditions and employment possibilities of prospective parolees; supervise and report parolees.

New York

Commissioner of Correction	Is responsible for prisons and prisoners.
Warden (or Prison Head)	Responsible to commissioner for care of prisoners, carries out commissioner's policies and procedures.
Parole Board (3 members)	Selects prisoners for parole and sets conditions of parole; may cancel time allowed off for good behavior; revokes parole if one member so desires; sets policies and procedures for parole officers; has no voice in the pre-parole training of prisoners.
Executive Director	Subject to the approval of the parole board, formulates methods of investigation and supervision; provides methods of recording investigations and supervisions; guides the work of the parole officers.
Parole Officers	Investigate and examine and report prisoners according to policies and procedures set by superiors; supervise and report parolees.

Ohio

Director, Department of Welfare	Responsible for work of all agencies of the department; permits each for the most part to set its own policies and procedures.
Parole Board (4 members)	Selects prisoners for parole and sets conditions of parole; revokes parole; may terminate a parolee's sentence at any time.

State and Official	The Most Important Powers and Duties of the Official
Chief, Probation and Parole	Works independently of parole board; is responsible for the work of the parole officers.
Parole Officers	Follow their own systems in supervising parolees; report to central office weekly; recommend when parolee should be discharged from parole.
Warden	Responsible for care of prison and prisoners.

IV. Officials' Terms of Office, Salaries, etc.

The following table indicates by whom the officials are appointed, the term of office, whether or not under Civil Service, and the salary in some instances:

State and Official	Appointed by Whom?	Term of Office	Under Civil Service?[1]	Yearly Salary
Mississippi				
Superintendent of Prison	Governor	2 yrs	No	$4,000
Assistant Superintendents	Governor	2 yrs	No	$840-$1,800
Prison Guards	Supt. of Prison	Indef	No	No salary[2]
New Jersey				
Member, Board of Control	Governor	9 yrs[3]	No	Expenses
Commissioner	Board of Control	Indef	Yes	$15,000
Chief of a Division	Commissioner	Indef	Yes	?
Member, Prison Board of Managers	Board of Control	3 yrs[3]	No	Expenses
Prison Heads (wardens)	Prison Board of Managers	Indef	Yes	?
Parole Officers	Chief, Division of Parole	Indef	Yes	To $3,000
Member, Classification Committee	Prison Head, approved by Prison Board of Managers	Indef	Yes	?
New York				
Commissioner of Correction	Governor	2 yrs	No	?

[1] Officials under Civil Service may be removed from office for cause only.
[2] A few guards are not trusties; these few receive a salary.
[3] Terms of office are staggered so that only one retires from office in any year.

State and Official	Appointed by Whom?	Term of Office	Under Civil Service?[1]	Yearly Salary
Prison Heads (wardens)	Commissioner of Correction	Indef	Yes	?
Member, Parole Board	Governor	6 yrs [3]	No	$12,000
Executive Director	Parole Board	Indef	Yes	$9,000
Parole Officers	Executive Director	Indef	Yes	To $3,000
Ohio				
Director, Department of Welfare	Governor	2 yrs	No	?
Heads and Assistant Heads of Divisions	Governor	2 yrs	No	?
Member, Parole Board	Governor	4 yrs [3]	No	$6,000
Chief, Division of Probation and Parole	Governor	2 yrs	No	?
Parole Officers	Chief, Division of Probation, etc.	Indef [4]	Yes [4]	?
Wardens (prison heads)	Governor	Indef [4]	Yes [4]	?

V. *Quality of the Officials*

Mississippi. With the exception of the prison guards all officials are political appointees. Most of the guards are trusted prisoners ("trusties").

New Jersey. The nine members of the state board of control and the five or seven members of the prison boards of managers are prominent citizens chosen for their interest in public affairs rather than for political services. Many are professional people—doctors, lawyers, etc. The Commissioner has had broad training and experience in public welfare work. His reputation in the field of prisons and parole is recognized throughout the United States. The heads of the various divisions are selected on the basis of ability. The classification committees comprise for the most part trained prison heads, doctors, psychologists, directors of education and industrial training, and field investigators. Parole officers must have the equivalent of a college education, two years' experience in social investigation, a knowledge of social case work, etc.

New York. The three members of the parole board are for the most part leaders in welfare, prison, or parole work. One is a psychiatrist and medical doctor with twenty-five years' experience in the state hospital

[4] Many are given "provisional" appointments, holding office at the pleasure of the governor.

service. Another was formerly a clergyman and chaplain in the army and active in welfare work. The third was formerly secretary to the governor. The executive director has a national reputation in the field of parole. The most of the parole officers have had training in social work; the majority are college graduates.

Ohio. Recent holders of responsible positions in the Department of Welfare have been political friends of the governor. No specific information about any of the four members of the parole board is available save that one was formerly a judge. The chief of the division of probation and parole is a political appointee without training in the field of his work. The parole officers are for the most part trained through experience.

VI. *Cost of Handling Prisoners in the Four States*

State	Approximate Annual Cost per Convict of Keeping Convict in Prison	Approximate Annual Cost of Supervising a Prisoner on Parole
Mississippi	$115 *	No parole exists
New Jersey	$550	$20 †
New York	$550	$60
Ohio	$200	Slightly less than $20

VII. *Preparation for Release of Prisoners*

Mississippi. Preparation for release consists in an attempt to so frighten the prisoner by his punishment that he will "go straight" when released. Whipping with a strap is permitted. The work of the prisoners provides little training for employment after release. Save for medical examinations, no studies of the prisoners are made. All prisoners, save those with serious communicable diseases, are mixed together.

New Jersey. All prison life—education, work, recreation—is a preparation for eventual release on parole. The classification committee, within one month of the prisoner's arrival, studies and reports on the prisoner from many angles, pooling its information and arriving at a program for training. A parole officer's report of the prisoner's home and social conditions is a part of that study. A continuous report of progress is kept for each prisoner. To facilitate training, the prisoner may be transferred to another prison or even to a hospital. A new program of training may be started at any time the committee wishes. A restudy is made every six months as long as the convict remains in prison. Before the prisoner is paroled, the parole officer who will supervise him sees him and talks over his situation, is sure that he understands parole obligations, and becomes

---

* Profits of prison products and use of "trusties" as guards lower costs.

† This figure does not include costs of classification committee, pre-parole studies, services of the board of managers, and keeping of records.

acquainted with him. Often the parole officer has assisted in securing a position for him.

New York. Usually within a year of imprisonment the prisoner is interviewed by one of the three members of the parole board or by the parole officer at the prison. The latter acquaints the prisoner with the conditions of parole. He checks the prisoner's correspondence to see the sort of contacts that are being maintained. A parole officer becomes acquainted with the prisoner's home condition and attempts to prepare it for the convict's eventual return. Records of pre-parole studies and investigations are kept. The parole organization being under a management distinct from that of the prison, there is no other systematic preparation of the prisoner for release on parole.

Ohio. No systematic training is given the prisoner in the conditions governing parole or in types of work suitable for employment after release. No systematic preparation of the community for the convict's release occurs. The central supervision office and the officer who will supervise have no knowledge of the case until the prisoner has been paroled. At that time the parole officer is informed as to the crime, dates, age and name, relatives, and place of residence. The prisoner's only instruction comes at the moment of release in a talk at the prison by the parole clerk and by the parole agent at the central office.

VIII. *Selection of Prisoners for Release*

Mississippi. After the prisoner has served his definite sentence, less any time allowed off for good behavior, he is automatically released.

New Jersey. When the classification committee believes the convict ready for parole consideration (after he has been at least six months in prison), the parole officer in the convict's home community makes another home investigation and reports to the committee. The various specialists on the committee also make new studies and reports. These, together with all earlier reports, are the basis for the committee's recommendation to grant or refuse parole. If parole is recommended, the conditions to govern parole are also stated. A special committee of the Prison Board of Managers then studies the recommendations and the reports on which they are based. The entire Board of Managers then approves or disapproves the recommendations. No one may argue in the prisoner's behalf. A usual condition of parole is employment for the parolee.

New York. When a prisoner has served his minimum sentence, he is eligible to appear before the parole board. The board has available the convict's prison record, social case history, psychological or psychiatric reports, reports of the prison parole officer, and reports of home and community investigations. Recommendations of prison chaplains, wardens, and friends are not a basis for the board's deliberations. No one may argue in the prisoner's behalf. Attending the hearing are the prisoner, the board members, and prison guards only. The board reaches a decision at once. A unanimous decision is required for release on parole. The policy is to parole a man only when he has a job waiting for him.

Ohio. At the end of the minimum sentence the parole board questions the prisoner and considers parole. His *folder* is before the board. It contains official data about the crime committed, prison conduct, arrest record, prisoner's statements to the board, and prisoner's story of his personal history. It may contain letters from interested persons. In rare cases it includes the reports of one of the four investigators of the board. Social case histories, psychological or psychiatric reports, and reports of the prisoner's home are normally absent. With most cases the board withholds decision for at least three months. Three weeks before granting a parole, the board must give notice of its plans to the prosecutor and the judge who convicted the prisoner. Weekly for two weeks a widely read newspaper of the area concerned must carry notice of the intention. Three of the four members of the board must agree before parole is granted.

IX. *Supervision of Released Prisoners*

Mississippi. Having no parole system, Mississippi does not supervise released prisoners.

New Jersey. Twenty parole officers have an average load of about 200 parolees. During the early weeks of parole the officer visits his cases often and maintains careful supervision. As the parolee becomes adjusted to life out of prison, the visits become less frequent, dropping gradually to four visits a year, to two, and finally to occasional visits only. The parole officer reports in detail to the central office which has available the advisory services of all parts of the Department of Institutions and Agencies. Although routine reports from parolees are required in special cases as disciplinary measures, chief reliance is placed on the officer's visits to the parolee. The parole officer works under the strict supervision of his superiors.

New York. No parole officer has more than 100 parolees under his supervision. During the first three months of parole, the officer visits the parolee at least weekly. The number of subsequent visits to the parolee varies with the behavior of the parolee, sometimes as few as four a year. The parole officer makes systematic monthly reports to the central office. He works under the strict supervision of his superiors.

Ohio. Each parole officer has an average load of 266 parolees. He works independently, following his own system of supervision. He reports weekly to the central office on the number of persons seen, miles travelled, and expenses. He has nothing to do with the systematic reporting of the parolee and need not see him at any regular intervals. The parolee makes a detailed written monthly report to an office in the prison from which he was released. There the report is handled by prisoners.

X. *Length of Sentence and Supervision*

In all four states the governor (or the court of pardons of which the governor is a member) may terminate a sentence by pardoning the prisoner or by commuting his sentence. Regardless of the system of releasing prisoners, 97 per cent eventually get out of prison. Under parole systems the average time spent in prison is longer than the time spent in prison under determinate (definite) sentence systems. For the United States as a whole the average period of parole is slightly less than one year.

Mississippi. The average length of time spent in prison is less than the average time spent in prison in states having parole systems. Since there is no parole system in Mississippi, there is no supervision of released prisoners.

New Jersey. Customarily all parolees are held under at least technical supervision until the expiration of the maximum sentence. The parolee must be discharged from parole with the expiration of the maximum sentence. The average period of parole is about three and one-half years.

New York. The law requires that all prisoners be under at least technical supervision until the end of the maximum sentence, at which time the sentence is automatically ended. The average period of parole in New York is about three and one-half years.

Ohio. The parole board may discharge a parolee (making him a completely free citizen without any restraint) at any time after the parole period has commenced. It is the practice for parole officers to recommend discharge from parole at the end of one year. Parole is extended beyond one year for cause only. In Ohio the average period of parole is slightly more than one year.